The Death of You

Also by Luke Sutton

Welcome to the Wonderful World of Wicketkeepers
(White Owl, 2022)

The Life of a Sports Agent: The Middleman
(White Owl, 2020)

Back from the Edge: Mental Health and Addiction in Sport
(White Owl, 2019)

The Death of You
Life After Elite Sport

Luke Sutton

WHITE OWL

AN IMPRINT OF PEN & SWORD BOOKS LTD.
YORKSHIRE – PHILADELPHIA

First published in Great Britain in 2023 by
Pen & Sword White Owl
An imprint of
Pen & Sword Books Ltd
Yorkshire - Philadelphia

ISBN 978 1 39908 605 9

A CIP catalogue record for this book is available from the British Library.

Typeset in INDIA by IMPEC eSolutions
Printed and bound in England by CPI Group (UK) Ltd, Croydon CR0 4YY.

Pen & Sword Books Ltd incorporates the Imprints of Pen & Sword Archaeology,
Atlas, Aviation, Battleground, Discovery, Family History, History, Maritime,
Military, Naval, Politics, Railways, Select, Transport, True Crime, Fiction,
Frontline Books, Leo Cooper, Praetorian Press, Seaforth Publishing,
Wharncliffe, White Owl and After the Battle.

For a complete list of Pen & Sword titles please contact:

PEN & SWORD BOOKS LIMITED
47 Church Street, Barnsley, South Yorkshire, S70 2AS, England
E-mail: enquiries@pen-and-sword.co.uk
Website: www.pen-and-sword.co.uk

or

PEN AND SWORD BOOKS
1950 Lawrence Road, Havertown, PA 19083, USA
E-mail: uspen-and-sword@casematepublishers.com
Website: www.penandswordbooks.com

Perhaps the deepest reason why we are afraid of death is because we do not know who we are. When a person does not know what they stand for and their purpose, they may be afraid to die because it means the end of their time to figure out these states of being. If you have a deeper understanding of yourself and your purpose in this world, you can greet death as the path to something more.

Sogyal Rinpoche

Contents

Contents

Chapter 1

The Road to Utopia

As I started to write this book, I also began a bit of a health kick. You know the usual – eat healthier/exercise more. With the summer looming, I think the look of my 'Dad Bod' in the mirror was beginning to frighten me. Anyway, while on my runs, or jogs (not sure if 'run' sounds a bit too athletic for that point in my health kick), I began to listen to some podcasts. The podcast that I mainly hooked on was *The Diary of a CEO with Steven Bartlett*. This podcast is hugely popular but for those of you who don't know about it, Steven Bartlett was the co-founder and co-CEO of the Social Chain (a social and digital media company) at just 21 years old, and it became one of the UK's fastest growing companies. At 28 years old, Bartlett became one of the 'Dragons' on the BBC TV show *Dragon's Den* and also released his debut book, *Happy Sexy Millionaire*. Guests invited onto his podcast have a wide variety of backgrounds, experiences, and learnings from life. I think you could describe all of them as 'successes', and many are entrepreneurs, just as Bartlett is. The podcast is brilliant in so many ways.

During one of my runs, I listened to the episode that featured the ex-boxing world champion Tony Bellew. It was raw and fascinating as Bellew spoke so candidly about his life and career. I would encourage you all to listen to it. There were a couple of lines that jumped out at me. The first was when Bellew described himself as a 'product of his environment' through having spent his childhood and formative years in Liverpool. Now, this in itself isn't any great surprise from a boxer growing up in a rough part of Liverpool; it is also a line that we have heard before from athletes, particularly ones engaged in combat sports. Essentially, Bellew described how his dad had been a fighter and had taught him how to punch at 12 or 13 years old. He had started fighting mainly to protect his younger brother from bullying because he was gay. Throughout this period, Bellew discovered that he actually loved fighting, and the story went on to him becoming a world champion. But there was a follow-up question from this section of the podcast that struck me as particularly poignant. Bartlett asked, 'And does this serve you now?' The answer was simple and quick in coming back from Bellew: 'No.'

In this easy back and forth between Bellew and Bartlett, a million thoughts flowed through my mind. This ex-world champion boxer was explaining that his environment had made him the best of the best in his sport, but asked whether this now served him or, put simply, helped him in his life now as a father, husband and more 'normal' member of the public, the answer was no. Bellew was enormously grateful for what boxing had brought him and was very open in saying that without it he would probably have moved into a life of crime. Boxing had secured his family's financial future, which he valued immeasurably because he knew that his children would not need to go through what he had. Nevertheless, in the same breath, he acknowledged that although boxing had brought him all of this, there was another side to the coin – he was a product of his experience in *all* ways, some of which were negative, and as we will discuss throughout this book, there lies the great paradox of producing elite sportspeople. There is a yin to the yang! I can hear you begin to argue that if you start fighting from a young age then that would create problems as an adult in retirement. You might ask, 'Where would that aggression go?' I get that.

As Bellew continued to speak, it became apparent that it was about more than just the actual fighting. He could always continue fighting on a softer level in retirement. He could keep training. He could keep in close contact with the sport, which he actively does. It was the type of person he had become through his participation in elite sport that was more the issue now that he was living a normal life. That doesn't mean he had become a horrible person – not at all; he is clearly a man with strong morals. Rather, he had been consumed by an absolute obsession to achieve what he wanted from boxing, and there was a cost to this. He openly admits to not having been a great father when he was preparing for fights. He virtually switched off from his role as husband and father and left it all to his wife. He focused on a particular path and no one was going to get in his way. But what happens when a person has travelled the whole way down that path and now has to enter a more normal life in retirement? Do they just flick an off switch?

All this made me think of Olympians, who I truly believe are special human beings. Their journeys are very similar to what Bellew was describing. I have been fortunate to have played sport professionally and worked closely with elite sportspeople from lots of different sports over a long period, and Olympians stand head and shoulders above others, in my eyes. They epitomise everything that sport should embody. In the highly commercial world of today's sports industry, Olympians are still the purest version of an 'athlete' that we have, and their journeys will weave through so much of what we discuss within this book.

I want us to start by considering what the average life journey of an Olympian looks like. From an early age, somewhere between 8 and 12 years old, our future Olympian will have shown that they have some special ability. At this stage, that ability might actually be shining through in a few different sports rather than just one, but regardless, people will notice that they are 'different'. If they are competing in certain sports, for example gymnastics, then they will be showing this ability from an even younger age, maybe as early as 4 or 5 years old. Their most obvious difference from others will be the pace at which they improve. While others take time to master a certain skill, they will conquer it and be hungry for the next challenge. They will have an insatiable desire to improve quickly, so much so that every practice session will appear as a huge opportunity for them to catapult their skills forward. They will also show signs of being highly competitive, but their ability to improve rapidly will stand out more than anything else.

As soon as our future Olympian has caught the attention of their coaches and their parents, it cannot be unseen. People around them will start to wonder if they are watching someone special. It will likely become a talking point amongst other parents: 'Have you seen how good so and so is?' People won't necessarily calibrate that they are watching a future Olympic champion, but if asked, they wouldn't rule it out. Our future Olympian won't be oblivious to this murmur around them. They will know they are different to their counterparts and feed off it – they will love winning and love dominating. The more they excel, the more they will want to do it again and again. They will grow in confidence as they continue to rise above others and receive adulation for doing so. Their family's life will focus on the sport they are committing themselves to – getting them to training, getting them to competitions, getting them the equipment they need, getting them the coaching they need – simply getting whatever is required. The sacrifices made by everyone around them will be significant and it will not go unnoticed.

Our future Olympian will also start to become very aware of current Olympians. They will watch them intently, dreaming of one day doing what they are doing, and talking about it incessantly with their parents in front of the television. It will become a full-blown obsession and they will tell everyone they know that 'One day, I'll be in the Olympics'. And everyone will either believe it or will come to believe it as they make their way through the junior ranks of their sport. Throughout all of this, our future Olympian will be laser focused on fulfilling their dream. Everyone around them will now start to invest fully in this too – it will become everyone's dream. They are all on the 'Road to Utopia', whether they know it or not.

By this point, our future Olympian will struggle to focus on anything else in life. Schoolwork and friends will be very distant second and third places in their list of priorities. In fact, all their major friendships will be formed around their sport because anything else is impossible. As they approach their late teens, they will be challenging or even getting into the senior international squads. There will be European and World Championships and Commonwealth Games, which will all be important, but in the distance will be one star shining brightly above all others: the Olympic Games. That is what our future Olympian will really want. Follow the yellow brick road towards the gold – the 'Road to Utopia'. Now as a member of a senior international squad, they will be receiving some UK Sport/Sport England funding to help them focus on training and competing full time. With the funding being broken up into bands of seniority and performance, they will begin on the lower end. In truth, the money will be derisory, the equivalent of less than £1,000 per month on which to survive. But our future Olympian and their family will know that this is the path they have to take – this is what is required. Even at the highest band of funding, they will receive no more than £30,000 a year, along with some decent tax benefits. 'It's hardly footballer's money!' I hear you say – well, our future Olympian knows what is involved and it does not make them any less committed. If anything, it makes them even more determined, because they are working towards an ambition held on higher ground than something as base as cash.

Then, one glorious day, a dream becomes a reality. Our future Olympian gets the call that they have been selected for the Olympic squad. What a moment! It is a moment that they and everyone around them have dreamed of for a long time. All the hard work, sacrifice and dedication has paid off – our future Olympian is going to become a true Olympian! They will be going to the greatest sporting event in the history of our time. The Olympic Games, born from ancient Greece and revived in the nineteenth century, was based on a love of sport, unity, competition and an ancient tradition of physical fitness. With such rich history and meaning, the Olympics glows with iconic symbolism. It is quite simply the greatest, and our Olympian is going to be there. After all the struggle and dedication, it is almost incomprehensible that it is finally becoming a reality. And we must remember: once an Olympian, always an Olympian. This can never be taken away from them and will never be seen in anything but the greatest light. We might hear someone down the pub say, 'Yeah, I used to play professional football,' and unless we recognise them immediately, we are already halfway to presuming that they had a trial with Accrington Stanley once upon a time, and that was about the long and short of their 'pro' career. But an 'Olympian' – now that is different! If you have actually competed in an Olympics then that is a badge of honour reserved for the very few and will always be considered something uniquely special.

The preparation for the Olympics will be intense. Paranoia about getting an injury will be matched by an intensity of training that aims to produce the perfect performance at the perfect moment. Our future Olympian will be ticking off the days in their mind until they join up with the rest of the squad. They will have all their official clothing and have tried it on numerous times in a bid to make it feel real. There will be little more important to their family at this moment in time. Every trip to the pub or occasion of seeing friends will immediately spark conversations on how things are going, how everyone is feeling. The build-up will be immense and there will be a realisation that it has been gradually gaining intensity over the years. The investment from everyone involved is enormous. Whether they recognise it or not, they are preparing for the biggest moment of their lives. This is when you can see that Olympians are the purest form of 'athletes' we have. They are not money-grabbing mercenaries, hungry for fame: absolutely not – they are elite athletes dedicating their lives to exhibiting their talents at the greatest sporting event known to man while the eyes of the world are upon them. So much of the sports industry has changed over the last hundred years or so, but the sanctity of the Olympic Games, and the Olympians who compete in them, has remained in place. It simply doesn't get bigger or better than this.

And while this is all in place, let's remember that for our future Olympian, the margins of success and failure at the Games are tiny. Depending on their sport or event, they might only get one or two performances in order to qualify for their final. Hear that again: after all this build-up, over years and years, they might have one go at making it towards winning a medal. Just one shot. Never mind sixty football matches in a season; our future Olympian has just one chance, and if they blow it then they *might* get another go … in how long? Four years' time! Think about the reality of that dynamic; it is actually mind-blowing. Many athletes have described the intensity of the Olympics as something that is incomparable – and is that any surprise? There is quite literally nothing like it and your chances of success or failure lie on a very fine line. No wonder it is an explosion of emotions for a human being.

Before I go on with the illustration I am talking you through, I am going to stop our future Olympian's story here. I am not going to talk through actually being at the Olympics and the results involved. Believe it or not, that is irrelevant to what I am trying to explain. That might sound strange but it really is. I have been fortunate to manage athletes who have won Olympic gold medals and others who have not performed well at the Games, and what I am talking you through exists for all of them.

I want you to take another moment to think back on our future Olympian's journey up to reaching the Games – everything in their life has been pointing towards it. And I don't say 'everything' lightly – it literally means everything they have done and everything that has shaped them so far in life. They haven't lived a 'normal' life up till now, they have lived an 'Olympian' life, full of focus and sacrifice. They have missed out on many things that other young people experience as life has slotted into a specific lane for them. And none of this has happened by accident or luck. In fact, it is the perfect opposite of that. Everything has been planned and prepared for over many years. That doesn't mean to say that there haven't been some setbacks along the way, but the years of dedication have all been pointing to one thing. And around that one future Olympian has been a family, a sporting club, and even a community that have all been on the journey with them, all getting more and more invested in it the closer it gets. There has been the shaping of families' lives as well – missed holidays, money spent on equipment and coaching, hours of driving to competitions and training, the list goes on and on. All of this is reflected in the tears of joy we see from parents when they witness their child achieve greatness at an Olympics. Of course, there is immense pride in those tears but they are also an outpouring of the sacrifices involved for all the family. Within the intense joy lies some intense relief – 'We did it!'

Now, I want you to ask yourself a question: Why do Olympians put themselves through this?

Here are some points to consider:

- The chances of success are small.
- The money isn't great.
- The sacrifice is enormous.
- The toll on your family is significant.
- The effect on your adolescence will be noticeable.
- The time available to do this is far more limited than for other sports arenas.

I expect that a couple of immediate answers to this will be:

'It just happened to be the sport they were good at.'
'They do it for the honour!'

Those things are likely to be correct, but the truth is that they don't get anywhere deep enough to explaining what the Olympic journey is all about. Nowadays we live in an incredibly fickle world. Information and change is available at the click of a button. Likewise, the adoration from young people of celebrities looking good with money on platforms like Instagram and TikTok has never been higher. Patience is at an all-time low amongst young people wanting more. Yet, in these times, there are still thousands of athletes desperate to take on the most honourable and pure journey in sport of trying to get to an Olympics. And the reason for this is because they have been conditioned for years to see the Olympics as the greatest possible moment of their life. This isn't some sort of sinister conditioning, but look back on everything I have talked about so far – the Olympics is positioned as the ultimate for this athlete and their family. Now, I am not in some sort of debate over whether this is right or wrong. In fact, I have an experience of this at the moment with my own children. As they show signs of development in sport, I can feel myself already looking ahead and wondering if a wonderful Olympic pursuit might be on the cards for us all. It's an intoxicating thought. So rather than placing judgement, I am simply stating the facts about how powerful this mindset can be for an athlete and their family. Within a future Olympian's journey, there is a constant inference that there is nothing greater that they can aim for or achieve – and I haven't even added the layer of going to the Games and actually winning a medal, let alone a gold. And remember, you don't just accidentally turn up to an Olympics. The process by which to get there is gruelling – it is brutal, in fact. There is very little space to talk of balance in life; you are either 'all-in' or you might as well go home. That level of commitment is required from the athlete and the family. Then, at the end of this, when you finally achieve your spot at the Olympics, the chance of you succeeding is lower than it would be in other sports competitions. The whole thing is as intense as you can possibly imagine in sport.

Our future Olympians go through all of this because they see themselves on a path to something great, something better than now, to a time when everything will fall into place and make perfect sense. In an instant, all the work and sacrifice will have been more than worth it – it will be in perfect alignment with their life's path. That is why I call it the 'Road to Utopia'. You see, the definition of Utopia is 'an imagined place or state of things in which everything is perfect'. I want you to take note of the word 'imagined'. Of course, going to an Olympic Games is likely to make your life a great deal better. A huge sense of achievement and confidence is good for anyone's life. However, the crucial element to this is, what is the underlying expectation for life after an Olympic Games? Imagine preparing your whole life for the designated 'greatest moment in your life' – what should come after that? Well, it wouldn't be a stretch to expect the greatest things. Let us not forget, this is not some school fair or the local village cricket team, this the Olympic Games – the greatest sporting event of all time, with a sacrosanct reputation. Your expectations for and post the Olympics are going to relate to that kind of symbolism. Now, I just want to repeat, I am not placing a negative judgement on this, and I want to say that because I sense there could be that implication from what I am saying. There is a great deal that is wonderful about this journey but we have to be able to see it for what it is and the conditioning it provides.

Let me give you a real example of this. As many of you will know, I work as a sports agent and manage a number of high-profile sportspeople. I manage and have managed a number of Olympians and have clients who have won gold, silver and bronze medals, as well as clients who have been to the Olympics and come away empty-handed. After every Olympics, I am inundated with emails from athletes returning from the Games who have won a medal, maybe even a gold, looking for management. After years of sacrifice, on not great money, culminating in an Olympic medal being hung around their neck and adoration from back home, it is not unreasonable for these athletes to expect that this is their time to cash in on sponsorship and appearances. Especially when you consider everything we have talked about so far in this chapter – it is the Olympics, after all! Sadly, this is not the real landscape that they face. The Olympic riches are for a small number and the rest are left disappointed. It is for this reason that I pass on the opportunity to manage many of the people who contact me after an Olympics. Unfortunately, I know how hard it will be for them.

That is just a monetary example, which is important, but not the whole picture of what I am trying to explain. Have you noticed in life how many stories depicted in books or films represent a journey to the promised land, not actually life *in* the promised land? You see, we spend so much of our lives trying to travel towards something better and more gratifying, and the

Olympic journey is this, but on steroids. The Olympic journey is a metaphorical charge to the promised land, but what happens when they get there? Does it live up to what is promised? Can it ever live up to what is promised? I have asked lots of Olympians to tell me what they expected from life once they had been to an Olympics and the most common answer is always along the lines of, 'Not sure, but I thought it would be great.' And you can't blame anyone for thinking this; after all, it is the 'Road to Utopia'. Yet, life is life, with its ups and its downs, its brilliance, and its blandness, and when athletes return from the greatest moment of their lives at an Olympics, how can what follows on not be anything other than a massive disappointment? How can we not expect them to fall off the edge of a cliff? They will still need to take out the bins and pay their taxes, and they may still have arguments with their other half at some point – life is life. This is something the everyday person lives with but if you have been on a path that conditions you to believe that life will be great when you get to the top of your game, then reality can be crushing.

If we truly want to understand the challenges of athletes in retirement then we need to grasp this point. The journey Olympians go on is unique but there are parallels in lots of other sports and sportspeople. Everyone is trying to climb some sort of Everest and when they do it, what do we expect? There is much more for us to delve into in this book, but the 'Road to Utopia' that Olympians embark upon is incredibly revealing and we have to understand all of it to understand any of it.

I will end this chapter with this. Arguably the greatest Olympian of all time, Michael Phelps, with twenty-eight Olympic medals to his name, was recently asked if he would like his children to follow in his footsteps in the Olympics. His answer was striking:

> Honestly, in a perfect world, I'd say no. Just because I don't want them to live in my footsteps. And I also know everything about it – I know the ins and the outs, the good, the bad, and the ugly. So, you know, as a parent, it just – it frightens me.

Chapter 2

Death

A ndre Agassi, on retirement from elite tennis, said:

It's like preparing for death. Nobody knows what it's going to feel like and nobody knows when it is going to happen and when it does, it's your time.

The Professional Players' Federation (PPF), which is the national organisation for the Player Associations in the United Kingdom, released the results of a survey they carried out on 800 ex-players. Here are their key findings:

- One in two said they did not feel in control of their lives within two years of finishing their careers.
- More than half have had concerns about their mental or emotional well-being since retiring.
- Loss of identity and purpose were common issues that led to more serious problems such as depression, self-harm, addiction, and financial concerns. It was reported that for many, retirement felt like a grieving process.
- Even the best-prepared athletes were struggling.
- A focus on success can hinder an athlete's prospects of planning for life after retirement.
- Only four in ten of those who felt they had an issue with their mental and emotional well-being had sought help.

- Fewer than one in ten former players had sought help for drug, alcohol, or gambling problems.
- Only three in ten former players were able to choose when they stopped playing professional sport.
- Just over half of respondents reported financial difficulties in the five years after stopping playing.

These findings were backed up by research from Xpro – a charity for former professional footballers – that claimed three out of every five Premier League players declare bankruptcy after retirement. And this is not exclusive to sports in the United Kingdom. According to *The Independent* newspaper, such figures are mirrored in American professional sports. In 2009, a report found 78 per cent of NFL players went bankrupt or suffered 'financial stress' within two years of retirement. Sixty per cent of NBA stars lost all their money within five years.

In the UK, an estimated 150 ex-professional footballers are currently in prison. Dozens of those have been convicted of drug offences after turning to narcotics following the end of their careers. Combine this with the bankruptcy statistics for ex-footballers and something is going very wrong. Yet, the rise and demise of the 'privileged' footballer makes great newspaper headlines. Most people are aghast at the money that footballers can earn and as a result, little sympathy is shown when we watch their lives fall apart. With little sympathy comes little analysis, and therefore, little understanding. It just becomes part of people's fish and chip paper. All these statistics are no great secret but they are nonetheless alarming and awakening. They illustrate an unavoidable truth: retirement is extremely difficult for the vast majority of elite sportspeople. However, how we understand and interpret this is the crux of the matter. As the famous American inventor Charles Kettering said:

> Knowing is not understanding. There is a great difference between knowing and understanding: you can know a lot about something and not really understand it.

As an example, the financial difficulties that face many ex-sportspeople are often put down to their overspending and the poor financial advice they receive. Granted, some of this is true but it doesn't help with understanding what is actually going on. As I said in the previous chapter, you have to understand all of it in order to understand any of it. We have to be able to fathom the nature and conditioning of elite sportspeople in order to appreciate why they run into these difficulties. As an example, a common symptom of depression is sleeping a lot. It would be like us saying that that person needs to be less lazy in order to help themselves out of their depression. Yes, physical exercise will help someone with depression, but that suggestion gets nowhere near to understanding their real problem and is therefore unhelpful.

Before I write any book, I ask myself why I want to do it. My reason can never be a monetary one because that isn't enough for me to make the long commitment of writing a book. As much as I adore writing, it isn't an easy process and it takes a lot of time. Money doesn't cover that. Well, actually, it might for some people but that doesn't work for me. There has to be something deeper to it. There has to be a profound reason why I want to dive deeply into this subject matter. Questions like, 'Why do I feel so passionately about this?' and 'Why does this feel important?' swirl around in my head. Putting this book together was no different. When I asked myself these questions, three specific answers came to mind:

1) I believe that the subject of how athletes struggle in retirement is one that, up until now, has been looked at in a couple of different ways. The first is the very base, soundbite approach when you hear lines like, 'He/she misses the banter in the dressing room' or 'They're just not used to normal life'. The second is a very technical approach on which psychologists have written some excellent papers. I wanted to write something about this that bridged that gap. Something that is simple and relatable but gives you enough depth to realise that this is a multi-layered and fascinating topic to examine.

2) I feel that there are messages within this discussion that can help us all. We frequently want to put superstar athletes on pedestals and I will often refer to them in this book as not living a 'normal' existence, but ultimately, they are just human beings like the rest of us. Their difficulties in retirement have lessons that we can all benefit from. Within today's society there are increasing numbers of people searching for meaning, purpose, identity and direction in order to understand what defines them as human beings. We will talk about all of that in this book.

3) Lastly, I want to give athletes a real voice in this. I have been fortunate to have been around elite athletes all my adult life and the many of them who struggle in retirement often feel unheard or misunderstood. They don't want to sound spoilt or overindulgent so tend to keep their

difficulties to themselves or only share them within an extremely tight circle of people. I want this book to elevate this conversation and make it easier for athletes to talk about these issues publicly. That might sound like quite a lofty ambition but ultimately, if this book helps just one athlete feel a little more understood, then I will feel I have done my job.

The first and very important thing I want to say is that the reasons an athlete might run into major life challenges in retirement are not straightforward, and they are not the same for everyone. I want you to envisage a smorgasbord of circumstances; individual athletes will relate to some of these more than they will relate to others. Some will share similar feelings about one reason but not another because ultimately, we are all different as human beings. However, there is an overarching reason that encapsulates everything within this – an umbrella over your smorgasbord, if you will! I am going to lay everything out for you in this book so you can get a full understanding of it all.

The second important point I want to make from the outset is that I don't believe planning your retirement makes as much of a difference as people think. This is probably a controversial thing to say when looked at in isolation so I need to explain it a little more. In many sports, but not all, there is a huge emphasis for athletes to think about what they want to do when their playing days are over. Do they want to take a course to help them with a second career? Or gain work experience in a particular industry? Or stay in their sport and take their coaching qualifications? Effectively, they are asked to have an eye on what could be next for them. The thinking is that if an athlete sees a clear path for them to move on to after their playing career then it will take away many of the retirement challenges. I agree with some of this and am in full support of anyone or any organisation that is trying to help athletes with options for them after they finish competing. However, I don't agree that it will take away all or even some of the retirement challenges that many athletes face. I also think it is a contradiction in terms to have a sporting environment that demands absolute obsession from athletes but also asks them to think about what's next – you can't have it both ways. You see, the reason elite sport is 'elite' is because the demands are extreme and only the best will survive in that environment. You have to understand the people you are dealing with. These types of people won't understand or want balance in their lives. In fact, their conditioning is actually all about imbalance – everything is tipped towards getting the absolute best out of themselves from their sport. You can create a plan for this type of person post-career but ALL they will care about is their playing career and that is why they are so bloody good. It reminds me of some quotes from Steven Gerrard:

> I was obsessed. Obsessed with being the best player in training every single day, and if I didn't, I'd go home and think about it and try and do it again the next day. You have to be obsessed. When you get that sniff and that little bit of hope, you've got to be obsessed to move them [teammates] out of the way. Once you're in, they're not coming back.

Do you really think Steven Gerrard was planning for something post-career with this type of mindset? Gerrard was fortunate to play football, which meant he earned the sort of money that gave him freedom post-career, but it was this exact mindset that made him truly elite. In one breath we demand this sort of mindset and in another we ask them to dilute it to think about what's next. The truth is that with an elite mindset, no amount of planning will prevent the challenges that person will face when you tell them that their time is up. You would also be mistaken if you thought this sort of mindset was distracted by money. Gerrard's mentality was about being the best, not about being the richest. That is a switch that doesn't get turned off by any amount of cash. So, what we will look at and discuss within this book are the real challenges that athletes face whether they have a plan for retirement or not.

I am going to use the stories of six ex-elite sportspeople to help explain this. They were all at the very top of their sports with the money, fame and adulation that comes with a profile like that.

- Matthew Hoggard, MBE, played for the England Cricket team ninety-three times and took 248 Test wickets, which puts him ninth on the list of all-time Test wicket takers for England. Hoggard was an integral part of the infamous and victorious England team in the 2005 Ashes series.
- Paul Walsh was a top-level footballer who played for England as well as clubs that included Liverpool, Tottenham and Manchester City. His career spanned more than 500 club appearances, scoring 128 club goals and one goal for England.
- Gail Emms, alongside Nathan Robertson, made badminton history at the 2004 Olympics in Athens. The pair won a

silver medal in the mixed doubles, which was Team GB's first and only medal in the sport.

- Tom May had a remarkable near twenty-year professional rugby career, making 380 top-flight appearances for Newcastle Falcons, Toulon, Northampton Saints and London Welsh, as well as gaining two full England caps.
- Johnny Nelson is one of our boxing greats. He is currently the longest reigning world cruiserweight champion of all time, having held the WBO title from 1999 to 2005. Johnny defended the title against thirteen different fighters, more than any other cruiserweight in history, and holds a joint record of most consecutive cruiserweight title defences.
- Clare Shine played professional football at every senior level possible including Champions League and International Football, and at 27 years old, could have been regarded as having the world at her feet. Instead, only two weeks prior to her sitting down and speaking with me, she retired completely from professional sport.

All six of these sportspeople were and are considered 'successes' and have had careers that others dream of. Yet, they all have an important story to tell around retirement from their sport. Their stories are different and similar all at the same time, as are their personalities. They give us a wide look at the sports world and what can happen when the moment of retirement has come. You are going to read about the 'loss' of many things, which is why I found the Andre Agassi quote at the start of this chapter so interesting. You are also going to hear about the feeling of 'falling off the edge of a cliff'. They are going to reveal so much to us because the real experiences of athletes are what we need to hear.

We need to absorb their stories in totality to be able to pick them apart and understand the entire dynamic. All six of them were remarkably honest, and as a result, their insight is incredible. As you embark on their stories, I would urge you to look for the differences but also the similarities in what they tell us. It is through their eyes that we will really start to see why retirement feels like such an enormous moment for an elite sportsperson.

Chapter 3

Matthew Hoggard (Part 1)

With 248 Test wickets, Matthew Hoggard will be considered as one of England's best ever bowlers. He currently sits ninth on the list of all-time highest Test wicket takers for England, which, in context, is higher than Steve Harmison, Andrew Flintoff and Darren Gough. There is no question that 'Hoggy' can look back on his career with immense pride.

While I considered who to speak to for this book from the world of cricket, Matthew was the first name that came to mind. I actually had a bit of a moment to consider why I was so drawn to speaking to him because I didn't really know anything about his experiences in retirement. I didn't know if it had been a struggle or a joyous flight path. I didn't even really know if he had much to say, which I guess made this conversation a bit of a risk. Nevertheless, something drew me to him. I played against Matthew quite a lot in my professional cricket career as we are the same age. Keep it quiet, but I once even managed to nudge around a century against him at Headingley! Throughout all this time, I got the impression that the rivers ran deep in Matthew. On the field, he was quite extroverted but off the field he seemed very quiet – a contradiction of sorts. He could be loud on the field, yet off it, he seemed happy just walking his dogs on his own in the meadows. He was also a Trojan of a cricketer, who would do anything the captain asked of him and appeared to have found his happy spot in life playing cricket. Ultimately, he seemed like someone who wanted a simple life and cricket provided that. There was something nagging at me as to how this type of personality was finding retirement.

> Michael Vaughan once told me that I was on the shop floor sweeping up after the likes of Harmison, Flintoff, and Jones. I just needed to make sure everything was tidy. I just needed to be constant and didn't have to be flash, I didn't have to do the superstar stuff. I've just got to basically be me.

That last sentence really sat with me – the role Matthew found in cricket allowed him to be him, which he loved. His rise to being an England star is a really unusual one. He went from being fast-tracked into the Yorkshire Academy at 18 years old to playing for the full England senior side by the time he was 23. He didn't play any junior cricket for Yorkshire and was in fact playing third team cricket for his club at 17 years old. Matthew was definitely not someone who was tipped for the top from a young age and didn't really have an immediate passion for the sport.

> I don't know if it was cricket per se that I loved. I just loved being active, loved competing, loved having the opportunity to beat people, I suppose. Football was actually my least love, but I loved rugby. I loved trying to beat my dad in the garden or cards or anything that we did. I don't know what it was. I loved ball games and the hand-eye coordination involved and being able to have that competition with people. And I suppose cricket is

a really unique sport. Although you play in the team, it's individuals versus individuals. That's what I like the most; [it] is that it was me against somebody else. Even though you have the support of the team, it was still you versus the batter or you versus the ball. The other ten people on the team couldn't affect what you did with that ball. Only you could do that.

Among the words that could have described Matthew as a cricketer were 'consistent' and 'reliable'. He knew what he was meant to do and would turn up every day focused on that. It was really simple for him – he understood his role and everyone understood how he would go about it – job done. For a man seeking a simple life, you can see why his life as a cricketer suited Matthew so much.

I'd always call myself a Shire horse rather than a racehorse. Or a Nissan Sunny car and not a race car. If you look at the race cars like Harmi [Steve Harmison] or Jonah [Simon Jones], they all kept on breaking down. They were brilliant when they were working but they were quite temperamental and things could go wrong with them. Whereas, as a Nissan Sunny, I didn't need that much maintenance, didn't need that much looking after – did the school run, the shopping and everything else, all the solid stuff. You'd let everybody else fanny about doing everything else, getting the headlines as long as you did your job well. My role, well, was to get on with it, quietly go about my business and keep out of the headlines.

This no-nonsense approach from Matthew was exactly why captains loved him in their team. Every team needs people like him because they form an important part of the steely backbone they need to be successful. Remember that Matthew was an enormous part of that infamous 2005 Ashes winning team that featured the likes of Andrew Flintoff, Kevin Pietersen, Steve Harmison, Ian Bell and Simon Jones, but there was one man who was almost always trusted to bowl the first ball of an innings for England in that series – Matthew Hoggard. Amongst those rock stars of cricket, that team badly needed Matthew. An illustration of how important Matthew was for that England team is the statistic that between 2004 and 2006, he played forty consecutive Test matches. That is a remarkable statistic when you take on board the demands of a fast bowler, but he was your Shire horse or Nissan Sunny – always doing his job, quietly and reliably. What was becoming clear to me was that Matthew loved the direction and structure that cricket provided for him. He knew where to be and what to do, and could be himself doing it. Yet there was one thing within his mentality that was underpinning all of this – self-doubt.

You know, I was a sort of person that never counted my chickens too early, never thought that I was supposed to be in the side or I was guaranteed to be in the side. I was always looking and listening to see if I had been picked when the team sheet came out. Even when I played thirty-odd Tests on the bounce, my first thought was, 'Am I going to be selected for the next Test?' This wasn't a feeling that I thought I didn't belong there – I wanted to be there and I thought I was good enough, but I just wasn't sure if everybody else thought that. That followed me throughout my career. When you look at the likes of James Kirtley or Glenn Chappell, who were around in my era, they weren't getting picked, and I was thinking, 'Why not? Why is it that it's me and not them?' I'm not saying it was a negative, though, because the doubt makes you need to perform every day, never lets you rest on your laurels. I never wanted to take a backwards step, always felt a need to perform the next day. I always wanted to earn the respect of other players, of my team. But feeling the need to keep proving yourself over and over again, it's a tiring thing – again, again and again; it's also a fantastic place to be.

Self-doubt is not an uncommon theme in many of life's high performers. Robert Hughes, the great Australian art critic, writer and television documentary maker, once said:

> The greater the artist, the greater the doubt. Perfect confidence is granted to the less talented as a consolation prize.

That voice in their head that tells them that they might not be good enough continuously drives them forward, even when all the evidence in front of them is telling them that they have 'made it'. It gives them an edge that the overconfident don't have. It's why they can be relentless in their pursuit of success because they are having a persistent battle within their own head. However, in the context of retirement from elite sport, I thought this was fascinating. In someone like Matthew, who found a home in elite sport, a simple life with purpose and direction, his self-doubts were given a place to be dealt with. There was a structure around him that allowed him to keep battling with them. Each wicket he took, each match he was selected for, was a dampening of that voice in his head questioning whether he was really good enough.

> You see, all the time you want it to be fun but every game I had self-doubt. Even when I was playing against Zimbabwe and couldn't get the tail out, then there was always a question in the back of my mind as to whether I would get the hatchet. Even in Johannesburg when I got twelve wickets in the Test, I thought I bowled like a shower of shit in the first innings. All the time there were doubts, always doubts in the back of your mind – 'Could I have done better than that? Somebody else has done better, am I doing the right thing now?'

The question that popped up in my head as I heard this was, what happens to this self-doubt in retirement? It can't simply evaporate now that the battles on the sporting field are over. And how do we expect that person to challenge these self-doubts without any structure or direction with which to do so? As Matthew said, this is also a tiring way to live your life; you don't really ever relax. So does this have an impact on someone trying to find the energy to tackle challenges in retirement? Or do the self-doubts simply overpower them now that they are exhausted after a long playing career? All these questions felt extremely relevant.

The truth is that professional sporting careers rarely end well. More often than not it is because someone has told you that you are not good enough anymore or too old, or both. All the while there is an athlete not entirely sure when or if they ever want to voluntarily walk away from it. The final years of Matthew's career were difficult for him, unfortunately, particularly the transition from being an England player back to being a county player with Yorkshire. Matthew was dropped by England during a tour of New Zealand while he and his wife, Sarah, struggled to cope with the arrival of their son, Ernie, who was a few months old at the time.

> It was horrendous. There was personal stuff going on in my life and I had gone to the captain and coach and confided in them. I told Michael Vaughan in the middle of a Test match that I wanted to sit down at the end of my bowling mark and cry. I just wanted the ground to open up and let me sit down and cry because I felt so inadequate, I felt so lonely, I felt so like a kid that couldn't get his ball off his dad and my dad kept turning his back on me. I couldn't get the ball. I was so frustrated that all I could think about was just sitting down and crying. And that's exactly how I felt. The answer to it all was that I was told that I wasn't being selected again on that tour. I headed home at the end of the tour and back to Yorkshire for the start of the season.
>
> I was still a centrally contracted player with the ECB but I was not selected for the first Test of the summer and I never got a phone call about it or how I was – they just abandoned it. I was dropped by England, which wasn't making me happy; I was now in a Yorkshire

changing room, where I didn't want to be. I was on the pitch, but I was only on the pitch physically; I wasn't there mentally. I was horrible in the changing room. I was destructive. I was taking energy away from the team and I didn't see it, and I couldn't see that. And my performances weren't great and I didn't care. It was just horrendous. No one spoke to me. Yorkshire didn't sit down with me and say, 'Okay, what's wrong? This isn't you.' So, it was a cumulation of the ECB not wanting to deal with it and Yorkshire not wanting to speak about it. I was left by myself being, most probably, a tosser in a changing room and on the pitch and not being fully aware of what I was doing.

It is obviously horrible to hear someone describe these sorts of feelings and my heart went out to Matthew as he revealed this to me. He was clearly crying out for help. Sadly, it shows how far professional cricket, in this case, needed to move forward in dealing with players who are struggling mentally rather than just casting them aside as difficulties, troublemakers or not playing well enough. This was back in 2008 and thankfully, since then, cricket has moved forward significantly in understanding and helping players with the mental pressures of the game. This part of Matthew's career did make me reflect on how the very place, i.e. cricket, that represented such a safe home for him, somewhere where he knew what his role was and where he could just be himself, could suddenly feel very different. Suddenly it felt unstable, unfriendly and lonely – that is a big change to cope with. Those self-doubts, which had created a positive effect on his resilience and determination levels, could suddenly start to run riot in a much more negative way. Was this an insight into some of the challenges Matthew might face in retirement?

Towards the end of the 2009 season, Matthew left Yorkshire and joined Leicestershire as captain.

> I didn't have any illusions or ambitions to be a captain, I was quite happy being a senior player in the background, giving opinions and not having the responsibilities of decisions. But this looked like a journey to help shape a club and I thought, you know what, I might just need some more skin in the game, some more responsibility, at this point in my career.

This is not an unusual feeling for a very experienced player who steps down from international cricket to county cricket to have – captaincy can represent a 'project' that gives them the extra motivation they need when realising that their international cricket days are over. I just found it interesting again, though, that there was this desire, or call it necessity, for purpose and direction in Matthew's career having lost it so harshly after being dropped by England. You can see how crucial it was, or maybe is, in his overall life. Earlier on in this book I discussed how elite sportspeople were products of their environments and how this could present challenges in retirement, but when you look at someone like Matthew, you can see that his sporting environment didn't necessarily 'produce' him, but more like 'grounded' him. The environment gave him a structure where everything seemed to make sense and feel easy.

After four seasons at Leicestershire, that retirement 'moment' came for Matthew towards the end of the 2013 season when, after coming back from injury, he travelled down with the first team squad to play Glamorgan away from home.

> Yeah, I was taken down to Colwyn Bay and got left out the starting eleven. I had just played in the seconds to prove my fitness and took two hat-tricks and twelve wickets in the match, but still got left out. That was the moment that I thought, 'Yeah, that's it, I'm done here.' I carried on until the end of the season, which was maybe another month.

After everything we had talked about so far, I couldn't help thinking that this would be a huge moment in Matthew's life. His home, his purpose, and his direction for twenty years was just going to stop dead. How would he cope with that?

The final day of the 2013 season, Matthew's farewell from professional cricket after a stellar career was Leicestershire's County Championship match with Hampshire at Grace Road.

> I didn't comprehend that message, that this is not going to be anymore, and I didn't take the last day well at all. We were batting on the last day and were five down. We knew that we weren't going to win and I was drinking Guinness at nine in the morning out of my drinks bottle. I didn't really understand the enormity of what I'd just done.

I could feel the sadness in Matthew as he said this. If I'm honest, I felt sad for him as well. You would wish that to be a true moment of celebration for everyone involved for what a wonderful career

Matthew had had. But was it a celebration or a mourning, or just a numbing?

One of the best Test bowlers that England have ever produced was facing a pivotal moment in his life, maybe like falling off the edge of a cliff, while trying to numb it by drinking Guinness. That feels sad to me but maybe if considering what's next feels too overwhelming, then just trying to pretend it's not actually happening feels better?

At the end of 2013, Matthew Hoggard was an *ex*-professional cricketer. That journey was over, whether he wanted to see it or not.

> It was probably towards the start of the next season before I really started to understand that I wasn't playing anymore. Because before that, it was the off-season when you don't do anything. Everything was just no, you have a lie-in, you do normal stuff, you're not looking for a job, you're just sat on your ass.

People would be mistaken in thinking that Matthew hadn't engaged with different organisations to try to prepare for retirement, though. He had sessions with a specialist company who were positioned as experts within the space of transitioning professional sportspeople into retirement, but it kept coming back to this sort of exchange:

'What do you think you want to do?'

'Well, if I fucking knew that I would be fucking doing it.'

The void left in Matthew's life was enormous. What could fill the hole that professional cricket had left? Was it even possible? A man yearning for a simple life was suddenly staring into the abyss of what he could do next, and importantly, what could fulfil him as cricket had done.

> You see, I knew cricket inside out. I knew what was right, what was wrong. I had to do what the basics were, how to get myself to where I needed to be able to perform. But now I'm in a game where there's no rules, there's no boundaries. I didn't even fucking know which part of this game I actually wanted to play because it's so huge. They say that you can do whatever you like but there's so much to look at, you don't focus on anything. There's so much you could do that you don't want to do anything. And then you try something and it doesn't work and you feel helpless. In cricket, we knew about executing our plans, do I need to change my plan or am I not executing it correctly? I can analyse that. I haven't executed my plans properly, therefore that's why I got smacked. Whereas if I executed my plan and it didn't work, then I needed to change my plan. And it's okay, you know what you're doing. But now you're in a game that you don't know what you're doing. You're not an expert at it. You don't know what Plan B is. You're all at sea and not knowing, and you haven't got the luxury of your teammates or coach around you. You can't just go up to the coaches and ask, 'What am I going to do now?' It's almost a voyage into the unknown.

I'm not sure if I can even make this comparison but this all reminds me of what I imagine an army soldier must feel like when they return home to retire from duty. They lived within a structure that made sense to them and now none of it makes sense. The interesting part was that I challenged Matthew over his need for structure and he pushed back on it.

> I hate structure, I hate organisation, I hate dealing with all the details. I'm actually really good at coming up with some idea that sounds really brilliant and then moving on without actually finishing it because I don't sort any of the details to do it and it ends up fucking up.

I found this interesting because there is a contradiction within it, because Matthew also said:

> I miss the ease of life. I think it's the best way to describe whether I miss professional cricket. I miss being told what time to turn up, what to wear, what we're doing right or wrong while playing a game that we absolutely love.

We chatted about it more because this concept of needing or wanting structure seems to be something important in retirement issues. I ran the theory by Matthew that maybe this was just exhaustion after a long career in which he challenged and dealt with self-doubt every single day. He never relaxed, he never took anything for granted, and scrapped for everything he earned in cricket. Maybe in retirement that switch is turned off and that person finds it very hard to turn it on again for another potentially long battle? So, a need for structure is conflicted by a lack of ability to get up for the fight again. Matthew gave me a different theory:

I'll give you another one – fear of failure. You see, if I say, 'This is what I should do and we'll be flying,' and you actually don't do that and you don't fly because I haven't done X, Y and Z, then you can have an excuse. Whereas if you say, 'I'm going to do this,' and you do it, and then fail, then what do I do now? I'm back to fucking square one. What the fuck am I going to do now?

I actually think that we might have been saying the same thing in different ways. Maybe the fear of failure had come into his life because fear had generally moved in so strongly during retirement?

I can remember laying down on the floor in my living room crying my eyes out. I thought I was a massive failure because cricket didn't end the way I wanted it to, we were struggling financially and I just didn't know how to get out of it.

Those self-doubts that Matthew had challenged every day in cricket through sheer hard work felt overpowering in a new world where the rules seemed to have changed. Throughout all of this, I never sensed from Matthew that he missed being a 'famous cricketer'. It didn't seem like any of that played a role in some of the challenges he had faced.

When I talk to people, I don't mention that I'm an ex-cricketer or anything like that. To me, cricket didn't define me and cricket doesn't define me. If you don't like me, then fuck off. Do not like me because I used to play cricket, because that is stupid. I don't know why, but I'm a massive fan of flying underneath the radar. My name is Matthew. If you want to get to know me, you can get to know me. And I'm quite realistic that I'm not going to get that feeling back of playing in front of 30,000 people at Lord's, and that's ok.

There is no question that retirement has been a massive challenge in Matthew's life that he and his family have battled through. That battle has taken the best part of a decade but he is finally seeing some light through it all with his business, 'Hoggy's Grill', which teaches people how to grill and offers catering for events. Sarah, Matthew's wife, does the business administration and Matthew does the cooking – and it works.

It's been hard work. But it's taken me eight to nine years to find something that I actually wanted to do and asked to pay my attention to and people say how do you find retirement? Well, I used to run around after a leather thing for a living. I now light fires and drink beers and talk to people like you. Not bad. I love cooking and I love teaching. It's not just a boring nine- to-five job. I'm now doing something that I'm passionate about again. We recently went to a 350 metres long by 150 metres warehouse and catered three-course meals for ninety people with food that I'd have been proud to eat myself. It gives me a buzz. So it's taken me a long time to find it, but I found it.

It was a fascinating chat with Matthew in so many ways and it felt like there was a lot to unpick.

Chapter 4

Matthew Hoggard (Part 2)

In my opinion, the disappearance of three things – structure, purpose and direction – is what had the biggest impact on Matthew when he retired from professional cricket.

I believe this is something we can all understand. Imagine getting your dream job – one that you feel you can be yourself in, know what is required of you and excel in. It might be a difficult job but in many ways it makes life easy for you. There is a clear path ahead of you and everything seems to make sense within this job. But then that dream job vanishes for you and you are still relatively young. You might have as long as twenty-five to thirty years left to work. What the hell do you do now? What can possibly come after your dream job? That void is both terrifying and suffocating.

Matthew found a home in cricket. Arguably, he could have found it in another sport or profession, but cricket suited him perfectly. He could compete doing something he loved by being himself, and in some ways, by himself. Remember Matthew's personality – he is an introvert.

> The thing is that I don't really like people. I'm a little bit of a loner living on the edge of the moors. I can take the dogs out and just walk for miles. It's actually why I liked lockdown so much; it was absolutely awesome! I didn't have to put up with the bullshit of other people, I didn't

have to speak to people, I didn't have to do anything. If
I could have earned enough money in lockdown it would
have been perfect.

This part of Matthew's make-up as a person is actually what
made him so reliable as a cricketer – he didn't get caught up in
the fake glitz and glamour of being a professional sports star,
he just got on with his job. Day in, day out, Matthew was there
following the pattern and routines that made him successful
while never taking anything for granted and never needing much
looking after. And also, to remind you, the thing that hooked
him into cricket as a child was the individual battles – it was him
against one other person.

And I suppose cricket is a really unique sport. Although
you play in the team, it's individuals versus individuals.

Of course, Matthew liked being part of a team and being successful
as a team, but cricket had a strong appeal for him because there
is an individualism to it. It was him versus someone else, and
he could just get on with it. Then retirement came along and
challenged all the fundamental blocks in Matthew's life that made
him so content while playing cricket. In his case, as mentioned
at the beginning of this chapter, I believe the three things that
challenged him were structure, purpose and direction. I will go
through all three of these, begining with 'structure'.

As discussed in the last chapter, there appears to be a
contradiction in Matthew wanting and not wanting structure in
his life. On the one hand, he 'hates organisation' but on the other,
he 'misses being told what to do'. The contradiction lies within

the dynamics of the structure. For example, it is the difference between telling the assassin who they need to kill and asking them to work out who needs killing and why. The assassin loves the structure of being told what to do and when, but doesn't want to have to create the actual structure he or she is working within. Clearly, this is partly dependent on character types and some might differ, but from my experience, Matthew falls into the category of the vast majority. Elite people always want a very clear understanding of what is being asked of them. Oh yes … and I did just compare a fast bowler to an assassin. To be honest, I felt like a few were trying to kill me over the years when batting!

Retirement appears as this black abyss with no structure, no rules and no clear answers for someone who has excelled at 'executing' a plan with a clear set of measurables to understand whether it has been successful or not. When Matthew described a 'fear of failure' as being a reason for not really committing to the work or details of any new ideas he had in retirement, I believe he was just describing a process whereby the abyss had made him overwhelmingly fearful of what was the right or wrong thing to do. During his cricket career, he never exhibited this sort of gripping fear of failure. If he had, he would never have achieved what he did in the game. Yes, he had self-doubts, but these were kept under control, or were even focused in a positive way by the work rate he applied to the structure and rules of the environment he was in. Like he said, 'I knew cricket inside out'; he knew what to do. Without that structure, those self-doubts can grow into full-blown, paralysing fear – in this case, fear of failure. It can manifest in an inertia of low energy, motivation and action in the person in question, hence Matthew's explanation that he would never follow through on anything. For people around this situation who are trying to help, it can be incredibly frustrating. They want to help the person, but they also want that person to help themselves yet it seems like they can't be bothered. They could be drinking a lot of alcohol and presenting themselves, for want of a better phrase, 'as a bum'. It is a vicious circle where those who are in it don't know how to get out of it. For the sportsperson drowning in the challenges of retirement, they can be bothered but they just cannot get past the gaping uncertainty that hits them once they have fallen out of the structure of their previous life as an elite sportsperson.

It is clear to me that sportspeople love structure. I can relate to this on a personal level even though I was someone who in retirement fell straight into business. Professional sport gives someone a very clear road map as to what to do with a day, a week or even a time of year. For example, I was a player who actually enjoyed fitness training but more often than not, we were accompanied to the gym by a strength and conditioning coach who would tell us what to do. At the very least, we would have a programme to follow that was written by that coach. Suddenly in retirement, I contemplated going to the gym and had this weird fear about doing so – what should I do when I'm there? Can I be bothered now that someone isn't there telling me what to do? I was meant to be an ex-professional athlete who enjoyed training and now I was behaving like a baby. This sort of example can apply to lots of different areas – nutrition, timetabling, even knowing what's appropriate to wear in a certain situation! I remember once telling a former client of mine, another ex-England cricketer, who had just retired, to wear 'smart casual' to a meeting we had together. As I said it, he looked at me blankly and I realised that he had absolutely no idea what I was talking about. He messaged me relentlessly in the build-up to the meeting as he tried to work out whether he had got it right. He was a highly successful ex-cricketer, who was 35 years old, and up to that point in his life had only ever worn cricket kit, casual clothes or a suit – that was it. Smart casual was a complete mystery to him that put him in a blind panic! I'm not suggesting Matthew had these difficulties but I definitely feel he faced a huge challenge when he was outside the structure provided for him by professional sport.

Let's move on to 'purpose'. Purpose is something that many of us search for at different points in our lives – is what we are doing meaningful? Does it give me a sense of fulfilment? Do I want to do this for the rest of my life? For Matthew, cricket absolutely provided a strong purpose in his life. He was trying to win games of cricket for his country and provide for his family – those are very powerful causes to work for. Patriotism and caring for your family would be significant motivations for many people. At the same time, Matthew would have been receiving constant acknowledgement of what he was doing. Imagine having a great day at work and 30,000 people at Lord's being ecstatic about it! It's quite clear that Matthew wasn't doing what he was doing on the cricket field for adulation but when you are searching for a purpose in life, knowing that something you do makes other people very happy really helps. There was clearly a financial element to it as well. Being an England cricketer means you are going to be paid very well, as you should. Knowing that you are providing for your family and that they are living in a level of comfort is a factor to add into whether you feel purposeful in what you're doing. There is one more element to mention: Matthew is the same as every other elite sportsperson – highly competitive. Cricket provided a glorious purpose to exercise this competitiveness. You see, he was competing on the cricket field to satisfy a competitive itch, but he was also doing it to win games for England. Being competitive can, by definition, be quite selfish – it often starts with 'I want' – but when that competitiveness is focused on a greater cause than yourself then it becomes a very effective way to let out all that competitive energy that sits within you.

In retirement, Matthew was left wondering what could replace cricket. What could be his next purpose? Cricket did have a financial element to it but that was only part of it – arguably, the smallest part. How was he now to find something that gave him that sense of a great cause? In part, this is simply impossible; you are not going to get thousands of people cheering you along in 99.9 per cent of other jobs! However, that doesn't mean there isn't another purpose out there to be found. The challenge for Matthew, as it is for all elite sportspeople in retirement, is that everything suddenly appears very 'transactional'. For example, his first job for a foreign exchange company would have felt very much like this. It's an exchange of services based on numbers on a computer screen in exchange for commission – there is zero greater cause involved so it didn't surprise me at all that he struggled in this dynamic. Even being involved in after-dinner speaking or sponsors' events will bring in money but there will still be a void in whether it feels important to do. The great giveaway in all this was when Matthew talked about how much he is enjoying his new grilling business, saying that he loves the teaching aspect of it as well as expressing his pride in serving quality food to other people. He might be introverted but he has found a purpose in what he is doing now because he is giving joy to other people and he can see it. It is different to cricket but there is a similarity – he has found something that now feels meaningful for this reason. Without finding something like this, elite sportspeople will struggle enormously with that void in retirement.

So, last but not least – 'direction'. Direction is where someone understands entirely what they are trying to achieve and why. Matthew knew what type of bowler he was, what he was good at, what he wasn't so good at, and what the team needed him to do. He completely understood the process behind what was being asked of him. Importantly, he knew that if he did things well it would equate to a successful outcome. For example, he knew that if he bowled enough balls in a certain area during a day, he would eventually get wickets. It was actually an extremely simple equation that he understood and had faith in. Likewise, he knew that if he put fielders in certain positions, he needed to bowl in a particular way, or that if he took wickets, he was likely to play in the next match. If the final result of the plan or match was positive or negative, he knew what he was meant to do next and why. There was a constant direction to what he was doing. In Matthew's case, this became even clearer because of how he was handled in his early days by the then England cricket captain Michael Vaughan. Michael gave him permission to be who he wanted to be, and furthermore, explained how that worked positively for the team. So, not only did Matthew understand what he was meant to be doing during a match, series or season, he also didn't need to reinvent himself or pretend to be someone he wasn't. He had a complete understanding of the direction in which he was pointed as a cricketer.

In retirement, there were suddenly no clear answers on anything. In which direction should he now point and why? And what if that doesn't work? Like he said, 'You don't know what Plan B is.' It is like he has been playing chess all his life and knows the moves well, but suddenly he's looking at the same chess board but can't remember any of the rules. Everything seems confusing and uncertain: 'If I do X and Y, will that equal Z? And what are X and Y anyway?' We can also add in Matthew's personality as an introvert – did he now need to go and 'network' to make a living? Did he now need to pretend to be someone else? What were people expecting of him? All of this would be incredibly daunting for someone regardless of the number of England caps they had to their name.

All three of these factors – structure, purpose and direction – go hand in hand. They overlap at times and if you struggle with a lack of one then you are likely to struggle with a lack of another. However, they *are* different and provide something for an elite professional that they may only truly appreciate when they are taken away.

Structure tells them what to do and when.
Purpose gives them an enormously powerful 'why'.
Direction shows them that if they do X and Y, it will equal Z.

After speaking with Matthew and writing up these two chapters about him, I fully understood what was nagging at me to speak to him for this book. The things that I could see had made him excel in professional cricket were the very things that would create challenges for him in retirement. I believe now that I could sense that from a distance.

What was lovely, though, was to hear how he has now found a passion and a purpose with his grilling business. It doesn't mean life isn't without its difficulties – there are good and bad days in everything – but there is definitely a level of contentment around this that has taken Matthew nearly a decade to find.

Chapter 5

Paul Walsh (Part 1)

Paul Walsh was one of the most talented English strikers of his generation – and this was during an era that included players like Ian Rush, Gary Lineker, John Barnes and Peter Beardsley. Paul earned five England caps, but there is far more to his story than what Wikipedia could tell you. That's why I always knew that he could bring so much to this book.

I first met Paul when he was invited onto a podcast that I was hosting a year or so ago. Both Paul and I are recovering alcoholics and during the podcast we discussed our stories, and importantly, our recoveries. There was so much for Paul to tell and I found it all fascinating – we could have chatted for hours. Paul and I have some similarities (yeah, the long hair at times!) but also many differences, particularly around our upbringings. Regardless of this, I have always resonated enormously with his story. Like me, Paul hit his rock bottom and learned to understand who he is in recovery, all while in retirement.

The lessons in Paul's journey start with him as a kid.

My dad was a West Ham fan. He didn't really take me to football because he was on the lash with his mates a little bit and I would have got in the way, but my uncle took me to Highbury. As soon as I saw the pitch and the stadium, I just fell in love with it. I was quickly obsessed with football but in the summer other sports came along like cricket, badminton, golf a bit later and even a bit of Gaelic football with the Irish community. I would play a bit of anything and everything. You see, there was a part of me that wanted to show off and I now understand that I felt a form of inferiority, because I was small. I was trying to get noticed, if you like, it was all part of that. So, I wasn't great in school, I just wasn't interested in any of it. I was fearful if the teacher asked me a question, I was fearful if the music teacher asked me to sing a note, I'd be sliding under the table. I didn't want to look stupid. I hated looking stupid. So, the only place I really got a bit of acknowledgement was when I played football, when I ran for the school, where I played tennis for the school or anything involving sport.

From the get-go Paul was fighting for attention and respect because he felt some inferiority due to his height. I have always sensed an intensity within him, similar to mine, and it clearly caught fire as he grew up competing in sport.

When I was 14, I played in these badminton championships and made it into the final. The kid I was playing in the final was much better than me and he was about 6 foot tall. But I was never going to lose that match, I mean never. I just kept getting that shuttlecock back. I would have to take two steps more than him to everywhere I went on the court, but I kept getting it back. In the end I just wore him down, point by point, and he couldn't handle it even though he was much

better and taller than me. Honestly, on the way home
I just stared at that medal and I was so happy.

You can see immediately how sport represented more to Paul
than just having fun with his mates. Every match, in whatever
sport, was a war because he was fighting to be noticed, and there
was nowhere better than playing as a striker in football.

Scoring goals got you noticed, it won the game, it made
you the main man. So I always wanted to be up front and
when you're my size, you have to be good technically,
so that's what I set out to be. I started playing Sunday
football when I was about 11 years old. At secondary
school I was playing football and cricket, and I tried to
be the best at everything. I pretty much was the best
at everything, except for running – there was always
someone who could beat me in hundred metres, always
someone who could beat me in cross-country, but I was
always in the top two or three.

The thing I resonate so strongly with about Paul is that, let's call
it, 'rage' within him, to be the best at everything. I had that as a
kid too. Calling it competitive doesn't feel strong enough; it is
something more intense than that. I wasn't short so I'm not sure
what I was fighting for but I also wanted to be seen and would
fight to win matches at all costs. The question, in a talented
young sportsperson like Paul, is what is leading what – is it their
talent or is it their mind driving everything forward? This will be
an important thing to consider as we go deeper into this.

When people say I was gifted, I don't think I was gifted. I think I worked hard on all of my ball skills. I used to spend so much time on my own with the ball dribbling, turning, knocking it, turning control. I did a lot of it on my own and I loved the fact that I could move the ball, change direction quickly and all the rest of it on both sides a little bit as well. So I didn't like being called gifted because I thought I worked hard technically right from day one. And so I thought I made myself into a player rather than being gifted into a player. Whether I was gifted with some basic stuff, I don't know. I don't know because I kicked a ball around with my brother and that seemed to start my anger, my anger problem, which has gone through my whole life. I used to blame my brother because he was two and a half years older than me, so he always used to get the better of me because he was always a bit bigger than me until I got to 16.

It is already easy to visualise the type of young footballer Paul was – small in size but tenacious to an extreme level. The fire within him was blazing and football was a place where it would play out.

Because of my size, there was massive rejection early on. I remember going to England Schoolboys trials when I was 14 years old. It was 1977, August. I remember that because I loved Elvis, a couple of his tracks, and he died in August 1977. We were at Loughborough University and were split into six groups at the end of the week – A, B, C, D, E and F. I'm in the E team! So, from there

I remember watching England Schoolboys, playing at Wembley, on the TV. England versus Scotland, watching all the kids that I thought I was just as good as. And I hated it. Hated it. It was envy, jealousy, every bad feeling you could have. I wasn't happy for any of them. Why is he there? Why aren't I there? I'm as good as him. That was my attitude.

Even Paul's home professional club, Charlton Athletic, nearly got rid of him at 14 years old because they weren't sure he would be big enough as a 5-foot 7-inch, skinny kid. But no one was going to stop Paul and at 15 he began playing in their reserves and was doing well.

I remember playing away at Fratton Park in a boiling afternoon and that was the manager telling me that I was doing well. I just left school and went and got a job, in those days you could go and get a job. Charlton already said I was going to be an apprentice. Between 14 and 15 years old, I'd overtaken everybody. I was training with the first team now, so I didn't want to be at school anymore. I was training with them guys and holding my own at 15 years old and then in that one year I became an England Youth International and things started happening quickly. I got into the first team and played a few games. We actually got relegated that season and the manager tried to protect me and took me out of the team when things were going bad, but then he got the sack and with nine games left and I played in all of them.

Throughout all of this, I wanted to ask Paul about how that fire inside him that was rapidly progressing him in professional football was playing out in normal life. The thing is that I know that fire can't be switched off, wherever you are.

> I was reckless. Yeah, I got in a lot of scrapes. People used to stab my tires, I'd get attacked outside the pub because of when me and my little group of mates used to constantly upset people when we were out. I had already created a bit of a name for myself locally. It was an egotistical, arrogant problem because I knew what I was doing with my reckless attitude, didn't I? I knew what I was doing so I kept doing it my way because to a large degree it was working. I was making progress. So don't tell me what the fuck to do. I know what I'm doing.

Paul had been fighting all his life to be noticed and to make progress in football. This rage in him gave him a method and, like he said, it was working. Sure, it was a bit out of control off the field but that comes with the territory. This was who Paul was or at least who he believed he was. Why would he stop doing what he was doing at this moment in his life? Paul moved on to Luton from Charlton and this is where things really started to take off for him. While there he not only made his top-flight debut but got ten England Under-21 caps, five full England caps, and was PFA Young Player of the Year. It eventually got him the transfer of a lifetime to Liverpool in May 1984 for a £700,000 transfer fee. He was flying.

But even so, it was reckless all the way through. People go, yeah, but everyone drank in them days. There was a level of arrogance and ego that went with all of it. So the more you got away with, the more you kept trying to get away with. It was the mentality a little bit.

Paul was definitely being noticed now. Everything he had battled for in his life was coming to fruition. He was now playing at one of the biggest football clubs in Europe.

I made my Liverpool debut against West Ham, my dad's team, and I score on my home debut in fourteen seconds and make the other two goals, and we win. I can't tell you the elation, euphoria of that moment. I nearly jumped over the stand; it's difficult to describe. But [the] thing is that I had to drink those feelings away because I couldn't put my head on the pillow with that euphoria going on without drinking myself to sleep. The truth is, though, that drinking was always the answer. I need to drink myself to sleep when it's good and drink myself off the deck when it's not so good. When it's all right, we have a drink anyway. So it's a drink, drink, drink around everything. Drink was always in the mix.

It is who Paul believed he was and what worked for him in life. A raging fire on and off the field. In the 1985/86 season, when Kenny Dalglish became manager, Paul had his best season at Liverpool with an amazing run of eighteen goals in twenty-five matches … but then there was trouble.

Eight games to go in the season and I got injured. My head went: 'Oh my god, I'm going to miss the Cup Final.' I didn't feel Kenny treated me very well and I drank – drank to console myself of what I wasn't going to be doing, and it just carried on for me. Anger, resentment, all being dealt with by alcohol, again and again. And over time, a year or so later, Kenny phones and says, 'We've agreed a fee with Tottenham and you can talk to them if you want to go.' You know what, I didn't really want to go, but I knew I had to. I went out that night with Craig Johnston, Nigel Spackman and John Barnes and I thought I'd lost my coat, which I hadn't, I was just too drunk to see it. So, I broke into my house, and ended up with eighteen stitches in my thumb. A few days later, with my stitches still showing, I went and met Terry Venables to sign for Spurs. We shook hands and I thought my stitches would burst, but I went straight into a hotel, single bloke on my own, and just carried on drinking.

By his own admission, Paul's time at Tottenham wasn't good. All that intensity that had driven him through brick walls during his life was now killing him. His drinking was escalating as his head was consumed with ego, anger and resentment.

I had a great opportunity. If there's anyone I need to make amends to as well it is Terry Venables because he actually gave me an opportunity and I fucking blew it massively. I blew it massively. Yes, I have a lot of regret around that because the first two years I was drunk.

I often couldn't make training on a Monday because of a weekend on it. I remember looking in the mirror now and then, thinking to myself with a massive hangover, 'Paul? What are you doing? What are you doing?'

I was never focused, never fit, never really professional, and I started to hate myself about what I'd become. And then my contract was running out and I was still very angry because I couldn't see my part in it. I still blamed other people. Like when I scored a hat-trick against Sheffield United when Gary Lineker was injured. Paul Stewart was the other striker and if I edged him on natural ability, he was always more focused than me. So Terry played Paul a lot. Anyway, in this game, I played up front, we win 4-1 and I score three and make the other goal. The following week when Lineker was fit again, I get dropped. I went fucking mental in the team hotel and stormed off to drink five or six pints with the game the next day. We won the game 1-0, Gary Lineker scored alongside Paul Stewart up front, so the win justified the selection. But I was fucking raging.

Moves to Portsmouth, Manchester City and then back to Portsmouth followed for Paul. He felt passionately about both clubs, particularly Manchester City, because it played a massive role in helping him build back his self-esteem after his time at Spurs. Despite that, a cruciate ligament injury brought his playing days to an end during a chaotic time at Portsmouth when the club went into financial difficulties and was then bought for a pound by Terry Venables. After all Paul's difficulties at Tottenham, Venables looked to get him out of the club as quickly as possible following his knee injury. There was one difficulty with that: Paul still had another two and a half years to run on his contract. Arguments ensued over money that was due to Paul from the club, none of which curtailed the anger and alcohol that played such a big part in his life. After the payments to Paul started and then stopped when the club went into administration, all was resolved when Milan Mandarić bought Portsmouth. However, Paul's time was up as a professional football player.

> I was so desperate to stay in football. I wanted to stay in the environment – become a coach, become a manager, but without any experience. I ended up becoming a football agent. Actually, over time, I realised I could never be a football manager because I'd be wanting to fight with a chairman when he talks a load of shit about why we lost. You notice there's anger attached to everything, absolutely everything. I spent the time being a football agent, not liking it, trying to get into TV, because I realised that the football opportunities weren't going to be there. I felt, actually, looking back on it, that was the only way I could replace my self-esteem, because the only thing I was any good at was now over. The money, power, prestige would only make me look good in the eyes of whoever. I don't even know who I was trying to look good in front of, but that was it. All the material shit that goes with it, look at where I am in life, all of that stuff, that was my mission.

Every time Paul spoke there was so much to take from it. His brutal honesty about how he felt when he had to retire as a player tells us so much. The very characteristics within him that pushed him to thrive in top-flight football were now unravelling him. His strength was perhaps now his weakness. Paul moved quickly into the building trade during the final years of his career. He was making money from it.

It was all about what could make me some money. Money, money, money became the obsession, because I thought money was the only thing that would give me any self-esteem, 'Look at me now, I'm not a footballer but I'm a builder, I can do this.' I always wanted more, because even when I had a nice car, I wanted a better one. Even when I had a nice house, I wanted another one. 'Where's the next thing coming that's going to make my life what I want it to be?' You see, fear crippled me now. I think that the only way I could describe it would be fear of the future. Fear of what I'm not anymore, not any optimism of what I could be, just fear of what I'm not.

Paul was still fighting the world, even in retirement. Fighting to be noticed. Eventually, this had to come to a crashing end.

I had an altercation with my son in an alcohol blackout at my dad's eightieth birthday party and knocked my mum over. Oh god. When I got off the pillow the next morning, I felt suicidal. And I'd felt suicidal before that, but I've realised it was self-pitying suicidal. It was all 'self', all about me – self-centeredness, self-seeking, self-pity, and self-delusion. I was obsessed with myself, my life, and my ego. And I realised that everything in my life was transactional. Transactional. What was in it for me? Nothing real. I needed help.

That was the start of Paul's journey of recovery from alcoholism and knowing that he was the one that needed to change. Not anyone else, just him.

> The best bit of therapy I had was from a hard-ass therapist in The Priory. One day I went to answer back and she went, 'Paul, shut the fuck up.' And I went to answer that, she went, 'No, Paul, shut the fuck up.' She said, 'You don't have to be right all the time. You don't have to have a reply every time. You don't have to get involved in everyone's shit all the time. Shut the fuck up.' It's the only bit of therapy I remember and when I now see something that's irritating in my life, I go, 'Paul, shut the fuck up.'

Paul's now over six years sober and working on himself constantly. He volunteers in a local rehabilitation centre for addiction and is trying to be the best possible version of himself. It doesn't mean life doesn't have its challenges or that he's perfect; he's still dealing with the scars of his past ways, but he's trying, and importantly, he can see where he's come from.

> I drove myself in sport and football, I drove myself into the arms of Alcoholics Anonymous. With my behaviour, my thinking, all of it. You see, it was my edge, my aggressive edge that got me everywhere. My aggressive attitude is what got me everywhere. I see some big

centre forwards and they've got no aggression when they get into the game. They lack that little bit of edge because they never had to have an edge – physically they dominated the space early on. Whereas it was different with me. It always had to be a certain way and that's the only way it could be for me.

And here is the crux of it for me with Paul's story and how he fell apart in retirement. Did the attributes that made him excel in professional football, which he knows he needed, actually eat him up and spit him out at the other end of it all? Managers would have loved Paul for his technical ability but more importantly for the street fighter in him – the lad that got into fights outside pubs because he was forever trying to show people that he was worth noticing.

Professional sport at the highest level demands an enormous amount from athletes and only certain types of personalities will survive in it for a long time, but what do we expect from them at the end of it?

Chapter 6

Paul Walsh (Part 2)

Persona is the mask or image we present to the world. Designed to make a particular impression on others, while conceiving our true nature.

Carl Jung

There was so much to take from my hour or so with Paul and there was definitely more he could have said. I relate very much to his story and also his recovery. As he spoke, it felt like a familiar tale to me. In my opinion, the greatest challenge Paul faced in retirement was the loss of his persona at that time.

From a very young age, Paul was fighting to be noticed. He felt some sort of inferiority due to his height, which created a war inside his head that made him want to prove to everyone that he was good enough to be seen. Yeah, he might have been naturally talented to some extent but the force behind him to succeed came from his mindset. What did he call it? His 'aggressive attitude' – that was it. That fire started in him at an early age but only became more ferocious over the years as people continually doubted him. Remember, only a year or two before he became Charlton's hottest young prospect, they were considering whether he could make it because of his size. Imagine what that did to reinforce Paul's mindset at that time to prove people wrong. Likewise, remember when he was 14 years old and he watched England Schoolboys on the TV play

at Wembley, when he believed he should be playing in that team
– there was zero balance in his mind about why he hadn't been
picked, simply rage, anger and jealousy. Over the years, his battle
against the world had layer upon layer added to it. Layers of
anger, determination and energy. Over time, those layers became
so thick that they were no longer just a mood or attitude thing
for Paul, they *WERE* Paul. The persona that Paul picked up at
an early age, and was then reinforced time and time again, was
of a fighter. A fighter on and off the field. Sometimes involving
actual fighting but more often than not just a way to live – in-
your face, edgy, reckless, raging, egotistical, obsessive, single-
minded, brilliant, and determined to an extreme level. Make no
mistake about this, those characteristics were exactly what made
Paul a top-quality footballer.

Paul's attachment to this persona was reinforced further
because it worked for him. As he said:

> I knew what I was doing so I kept doing it my way
> because to a large degree it was working. I was making
> progress. So don't tell me what the fuck to do. I know
> what I'm doing.

He could see that he had a method to being successful in life,
or more like an attitude to being successful in life, so who was
to tell him that was wrong? There is another layer to add on to
this as well. Paul's 'success' in life was that of an elite footballer,
so consider what that involved: firstly, significant amounts of
money, and secondly, the most intense euphoria of doing his job
in front of tens of thousands of live fans in a stadium bouncing
with passion and emotion. As he said when he scored on his

Liverpool debut, 'I nearly jumped over the stand, it's difficult to describe.' So, Paul had a way to live his life that created extreme rewards, ones that other people dream of, and he did this for a very long time. All of this meant that by the time Paul reached the end of his playing days, that persona of 'Paul Walsh' was well and truly embedded in him regardless of what was next for him in life. This is a position that many professional sportspeople unknowingly find themselves in when retirement looms. I say 'unknowingly' because they are not consciously considering a different approach to life in retirement. Why would they? It has seemingly worked all their life up till now so it's going to be more of the same but just not as an active professional athlete. It is also where the ego takes on a huge role. This sort of persona is largely driven by the ego wanting to look like the 'the big I am'. The real driver behind it is actually fear – fear that people won't like them, rate them, or want to be associated with them. The persona puts on a big, confident, aggressive or humorous front to make sure that people don't see any of the fear underneath. Remember Carl Jung's quote at the start of this chapter – persona is a mask to make a particular impression. Paul's aggressive attitude was going with him into retirement regardless of the consequences.

I talked a lot about this subject in my first book, *Back from the Edge*, because it played a huge part in my downfall and spiral into addiction. In my recovery I have had to learn to let go of the persona I thought that people wanted to see and instead start to live with the real me, warts and all! Up to that point, my life was consumed by trying to show a certain impression of me to people regardless of how much it was hurting me. It was insanity, but sadly, many professional sportspeople struggle with this. In the book, I highlighted Paul Gascoigne or, as everyone, including himself, calls him, 'Gazza'. Gazza is a persona – a funny, heavy drinking, lad next door – but I think the truth is that Paul Gascoigne wants to be a very different person to Gazza. He lives in pain and fear but can't let go of the act that he has to play in being Gazza because that is what he thinks people will only like and will only make him successful. Even in the face of disaster after disaster, he can't let go of Gazza and wants to carry on being that person to people. It's why I would never buy a ticket to watch him in an after-dinner question and answer session. That is him just playing up to the character called Gazza but actually he needs to be getting help and stepping away from that altogether. Mine and Paul Walsh's stories are nowhere near as high profile as Paul Gascoigne's but it is all the same thing. We walked into retirement with the same attitude that had made us successful in professional sport but was starting to kill us outside of it.

You might ask, 'Doesn't that attitude work in real life to be successful?' Well, let's have a think about it with Paul Walsh. Anger flowed through him ever since he was a kid – it's fair to say it was a constant. He channelled it into football because he was on a lifelong mission to be noticed and ultimately, to win. There was nowhere better to do this than scoring goals. He could be the main man where everyone could see him and he could get the respect he had fought for all his life. That anger was a powerful driver in getting the best out of him but it was a fine line. Paul fell out with managers, teammates, people in the pub – it was never far from him. But football protected this because ultimately, he was judged by his football. If he was scoring goals and the team was winning, all was ok – even better than that, all was good. It is the great disease of professional sport. Results are what truly matter to everyone involved – by and large, that's it. But importantly, that isn't real life. You can't behave like that in the real world, especially when you are no longer 'special'. You are now an *EX*-footballer and people are not going to put up with that sort of attitude or behaviour. They won't want to be around you or work with you or be your friend. Even your family in this situation will start to push back against you. Yet, for Paul, it was exactly *this* attitude that had made him be successful and got him noticed in the first place and now the world was telling him the opposite. So, what did he do? He searched for things that would bring him back to that status of being 'the big I am', of being 'special'. I want to highlight this quote from Paul because it is so telling in everything that I have just spoken about.

> You see, fear crippled me now. I think that the only way I could describe it would be fear of the future. Fear of what I'm not anymore, not any optimism of what I could be, just fear of what I'm not.

You can see how the reality of retirement hit Paul hard. The persona he thought he was, he thought he needed to be, that had worked for him in the past, was now under serious attack. How could he find a way to regain that position his persona had within football of looking successful and on top of life? What came next was a scramble for more money and all the material showings that came with it so that he could show the world that everything was in hand – Paul Walsh was still Paul Walsh! His pursuit of being on television was part of this, as was his angry reaction when that came to an end. The ego of his persona was never going to accept any of these things. And all of this is attached to how Paul defined himself at that time. He defined himself by visual successes – money, houses, fame etc.; everything was external. Appearing successful and strong was vitally important to Paul at this stage in his life because it was the persona that had helped him to survive and thrive as a professional footballer. He was still just that young kid fighting to be seen.

All the while, Paul's friend, alcohol, was alongside him. Again, this is very similar to my story. Alcohol was a great friend for Paul and me – it came with us everywhere and for every occasion. We drank when we were happy, sad, bored, or anything in between. And the reason for it was that it quieted our heads. That fire within us that drove us to push ourselves to the limit and beyond was hard to live with. It created extreme emotional reactions. Sometimes this meant good things and sometimes this meant bad things. Remember Paul's quote when he scored on his Liverpool debut:

> I can't tell you the elation euphoria of that moment.
> I nearly jumped over the stand, it's difficult to describe.
> But thing is that I had to drink those feelings away
> because I couldn't put my head on the pillow with that
> euphoria going on without drinking myself to sleep. The
> truth is, though, that drinking was always the answer.

Unfortunately, alcohol just bolsters the illusions that your ego tells you about who you need to be and what people want from you – the persona!

Paul's rock bottom was a very serious rock bottom in punching his son. You only needed to hear the emotion in him as he told the story. But sadly, that was what was needed to make him stop and think about whether his attitude to life that had been his 'method' to success was working anymore. Did anger play a healthy or unhealthy role in his life? Did he make good decisions when his ego was in control? Why was he so worried about what people thought about him? Did alcohol help any of this? What was he so fearful of? These were very hard questions for him to confront but they were the start of him changing his life to be the man he is trying to be today – a better husband, father, son, friend, and man. The fact that he used to play professional football is irrelevant to any of that.

Paul's struggle with an attachment to the persona he thought he was is very common in professional sportspeople when they retire. It can manifest itself in different ways and for Paul, alcohol was a big part of it. Ultimately, this struggle exists because they want to hold on to their old self that made them so successful in their sport but now the rules seem to have changed for them in the outside world. Sometimes, as with Paul, it takes a total breakdown to let go of that old persona to begin to learn how to live a happy life outside the bubble of professional sport. If that process of letting go doesn't happen, then unfortunately, there will be a continual struggle because the life of a professional sportsperson is not real to the normal world.

Paul's letting go of his old ways is a work in progress, as it is with me, but the crucial part is that it is underway. His story is powerful in so many ways, as is his brutal honesty in now confronting it. Professional football didn't make this all happen for Paul; he was made for professional football, but crucially, the sport rewarded him for it, but eventually, in retirement, that all fell apart.

Chapter 7

Gail Emms (Part 1)

Gail Emms and Nathan Robertson made badminton history at the 2004 Olympics in Athens. The pair won a silver medal in the mixed doubles, which was Team GB's first and only medal in the sport. It was a moment that I actually remember vividly – a classic Olympic Games moment, whereby suddenly I was completely enthralled by a sport that I hadn't ever previously paid much attention to in my life. I remember the power and energy of Gail Emms and the grace of Nathan Robertson on court – they were a brilliant pair. I was then and still am in absolute awe of people who reach the top of a sport in which there is very little or zero history of success in their home nation. It's one thing adding a medal to a country's long line of success in that sport but it really is something else when you achieve it from seemingly nowhere. In that instance, you are a true history maker, a trailblazer that future generations within the sport will benefit from. That is exactly what Gail Emms and Nathan Robertson were for badminton. The pair also went on to win gold at the 2006 World Championships in Madrid and to be ranked number one in the world. Why badminton in this country was never able to build on what the pair achieved is for another book but needless to say, it was and is a disgrace.

Before we start looking at Gail's journey into, through and, most importantly, out of badminton, I want us to roll the tape forward to when she reached retirement in her early thirties. By any measurement, Gail was a huge sporting success for Great Britain but this is how she ended up:

> I just remember thinking, what was the point? I hate saying this, I started to resent the sport. What was the point of doing what I did? What was the point of playing? What was the point? Because I was like, look at me. It was all supposed to be a good thing. It was supposed to be my dream and yet I can't go anywhere. No one wants me, I don't even know what the hell to do. I don't even know what to do about money. I don't even know what to do about anything – I felt completely lost. Lost is not good for me. And I just remember thinking that the worst thing is that I love my friends and family but they just didn't get it. I remember my partner at the time being like, 'But you've won an Olympic medal, just be happy.' People don't get it and that's what's so heartbreaking about it. I was angry but not angry at any one person, more the system. Angry at the conveyor belt I was put on. That's all you are. You're not a person. I lost who I was as I became a robot badminton player.

Gail's story is heartbreakingly revealing and the emotion that flowed out of her as she spoke to me over a decade after retiring showed how intense her feelings had been during that time. She was recalling it as if it had happened the week before. The truth is that if we are not able to learn from Gail's experiences in this book then I haven't done a very good job. But as with everyone, we need to understand Gail's journey within badminton to really understand how she felt in retirement. There's no doubt her entry into the sport was a unique one.

My mum was one of the first football Lionesses and played in the first Women's World Cup in 1971 in Mexico. She was part of the 'Maverick Team' at 19 years old. The FA were asked to send a women's team to this World Cup and actually said no because they said women shouldn't be playing football. Regardless of that, the Maverick Team was put together, including my mum, and she played in front of 85,000 people in the Azteca Stadium and scored two goals. When she got home, the FA banned her for six months and the coach was banned for life for going out there.

So my mum was just an incredible footballer, but the amount of abuse that she got was off the scale. Every time she went to play football, she was shouted at and abused, like 'get in the kitchen' and all that kind of stuff. So, when I came along and I'm the eldest, my mum didn't want me to go into football because she didn't want me to go through what she went through. It was basically in her mind that I'm going to find another sport for my daughter but back in the seventies and eighties, there weren't pathways or girls teams. There was nothing really promoting girls' sport. So, I spent my childhood just running around after my mum, basically looking for a sport for me to get into. Eventually, there was a tin hut badminton hall at the end of our road, around the corner. It had tennis courts outside and badminton inside in this tin hut and that was it. My mum and dad were members and I started playing from the age of about 3 or 4 years old.

The way in which Gail ended up being an elite badminton player was more about pragmatism than an adoration of the sport. It was a sport that her mum found for her.

> I don't think I can ever truly say 'I love badminton', which I think shocks a few people. I just loved being good at something. I've got memories of when I was 7 years old and playing in an under-11s tournament and I got to the final. I remember all the other girls going, 'Wow, who is this girl?' It was more about that for me – very much about the adulation. If I look back at it, it was never about 'Oh my God, I did this great shot in the final set'. I just loved that feeling of people knowing I was really good at badminton. It was more of a process for me. If you talk to Nathan [Robertson], he's very much about the love of the game. You could tell this in the style of our play – he was a very natural player, very Federer, and my game, I just whacked it really hard!

Despite starting in the sport at an early age, Gail's progress on an elite world level was, in comparative terms, quite late, but this was as much about how immature elite level badminton was in the UK in the nineties. She and Nathan Robertson reached the semi-finals of the 1994 World Junior Championships held in Kuala Lumpur and ended up with a bronze medal. In 1998, after graduating from Kingston University, Gail became a full-time professional badminton player with the help of National Lottery funded grants paid to her by UK Sport. Now all roads pointed towards the Olympics and in 2004 that became a reality. The Athens Olympics of that year were enormous for Gail in so many ways. It was her first Olympics and she was 27 years old. After years of sacrifice, it was the first time she truly felt she had hit the big time in sport. The range of emotions in Athens were to be as intense as they could come.

> Yeah, and we weren't expected to get a medal as well. But, as you know, in the Olympics, anything can happen. The number one seeds, who hadn't lost for three years, basically lost their bottle in the quarter-finals and lost. We then realised that we would have to play the Danish pair in the semi-finals and we had always beaten them. We knew we were going to be in the final because, we thought, we're not losing to them. It was the rollercoaster of everything. One minute you walk around the Olympic Village and feel that massive pride and then suddenly, it was like, 'Holy shit, we're actually going to win a medal here.'

In the end, Gail and Robertson were only three points away from winning gold in the final but they still made history. It should have been a game-changing moment for British badminton, but it was certainly a life-changing moment for both of them. Nothing would ever be the same.

> We were still struggling to process everything because we were actually still gutted that we'd lost gold, but next

thing you know, we were going to parties and TV shows. Suddenly it was a massive release. When you've been so focused for so long and sacrificed so much, it's like it is all built up in you, and then you have this opportunity to release it and it's like opening a floodgate! Nathan and I are very party people, very extroverted, and we loved it! And you know what, there was a bit of ego in it all. For years I would go into bars and restaurants and people couldn't care less that I played badminton but suddenly people would recognise me say, 'Oh my god, I saw your match. Oh my god, you're amazing.' I loved getting that adulation.

Gail's immediate honesty about how adulation and ego played a role in her story was so refreshing. I often think that the word 'ego' makes people cringe a little but understanding how it helps and hurts an elite athlete is vital in what we are looking at. I'm going to talk about this more in the next chapter.

After six months of partying, Gail and Robertson did get back to training, and 2005 and 2006 were outstanding years for them as they reached the top of the world rankings. All the focus was now on the 2008 Beijing Olympics, in which they would be approaching as firm medal contenders. The whole experience was very different to Athens, though, and suddenly, Gail got an immediate look at the system or 'conveyer belt' that she was unknowingly part of.

Beijing was horrible. There's a lot more expectation. Nathan had an operation because his ankle was knackered, basically. There were a lot of funding issues.

We had people coming up to us going, 'If you don't win a medal, my job is gone.' It was nasty. I don't look back at those Olympics in any fun way. It didn't feel the same as Athens at all. There was the excitement of Athens, and Beijing just felt like a military camp. Even Team GB camp didn't feel so great. It was clear that we were there to win medals and the enjoyment just zapped out of me. The enjoyment of being a sportsperson just wasn't there anymore. It felt like, 'You have to do this job, you have to get a medal, otherwise you're a failure.'

The pair came away medal-less from Beijing but actually played really well. In the first round they were drawn against the Chinese pair, who were the gold medal favourites and the poster pair of the tournament, and beat them. But they lost to the South Korean pair in the quarter-finals who went on to win gold. Where they had benefitted from a favourable route into the final in Athens, Beijing had thrown them the toughest of routes. For Gail, that was it, it was time to retire.

After Beijing, I thought, 'I can't do any more.' I just remember thinking, 'I'm the fastest and strongest I can be. I'm 31 years old, I cannot be any better than I am … and I've just lost, so fair play, it's time to retire.'

The start of retirement was very similar to the experience Gail described after Athens – a release.

I had three months where I just basically ate and partied a lot. I could do whatever I wanted. It was like a dream.

After being told what to do, what to eat, what to wear, where to be, I suddenly felt like I was sticking two fingers up to it all, even though there wasn't anyone to stick two fingers up to! You see, you revert back to a kid stage. I would say in sport that the dynamic with the coaches is that they are the adult and you are the child. That's the way they control you. They treat you like kids. You know, it's like a parent–child situation. If you do something wrong, you're punished for it. When I retired, I reverted back to being a kid even though I was in my early thirties because I didn't have an adult there to guide me through it. It's like the routine of the school day, and then suddenly it's the summer holidays. That's it. And then after six weeks of summer holidays, you're actually begging for school because at least you know where your place is. You know what to do. You've got a purpose. That is literally like how it is but in retirement you don't feel like the summer holidays have ended. It was just so bizarre and I felt lost.

Gail became a mum fairly quickly in retirement and some might have thought that would have helped her with a sense of stability but it was more complicated than that. As she battled to understand what 'normal' was in retirement, motherhood suddenly thrust her into the most traditional of 'normal' roles without much preparation time. As much as she wanted children, it wasn't going to calm many of the challenges she was starting to face.

The thing is, I still wanted to find another career, but I remember going to meetings and I didn't know what

I was doing. I had the CV of an 18-year-old and I didn't understand anything. I had no idea. Literally, not a clue. I just remember going into these meetings thinking that I didn't actually know what they were talking about. It was just meeting after meeting without any sort of decision on anything. Everyone would sound really positive after it but then it'd not go anywhere. I couldn't cope with it. In badminton, I know where I ranked. In the real world, I had no idea where I ranked. And for my ego, I didn't know how to handle it. For my ego to walk in somewhere, I had no idea if I was better than that person or not. I knew I could beat them at badminton, but I had no idea if I was better than them in the world of marketing or sales. It freaked me out. I had no idea where I stood. And also feedback as well… feedback?! No one gives you feedback. I would go for an interview for a job and then they just go, 'Okay, sorry, you didn't get it', and I would be left with – Tell me why? How can I improve? How am I supposed to get better if you don't tell me? As a sportsperson, we are used to being told what we're shit at and how we need to improve it. I'm good with that but with this, it was just nothing.

The raw emotion in Gail as she talked through this was powerful. Her sense of loss was inescapable and it reminded me about a previous quote from her that I had read: 'I thought I was ready to retire but the grief I felt was visceral.'

No one talks about it. And it was only a few years later that someone showed me the Grief Curve and it just hit me and I went, 'That's it!' You have to grieve. And no one talked to me about grieving your identity, grieving your sport, grieving because you have to say goodbye. You have to, and you have to do it in the right way. And it's heart-breaking. And I know some people say sportspeople die twice, but you do. You really do. It's been my heart. You can't not put your heart and soul into being an athlete. You have to because if you don't, you'll get found out, right? So if you don't put everything into your match or your sport, you will get found out. That was me since 3 or four 4 old, I've been doing my sport, calling myself a badminton player.

As Gail talked, she cried. Real emotion poured out of her as if it had all happened just the other day. In many ways, it felt like she was still grieving.

Purpose. Yeah, purpose, which has been a massive motivation for me, and I had to grieve that. Don't get me wrong, I'm used to starting back at the bottom and I'm working my way up. But walking into a room and saying, 'Hi, I'm Gail, I'm an Olympic badminton player', even that, I couldn't say that. People don't realise how much those words meant to me for status. I know, it's ego, but it's not a bad word. It's a great word. When you've had all those years of believing in yourself and getting to that point, and then suddenly it's all gone.

The topics of ego and status are so important for the discussion within this book, and as I've already said, Gail's honestly on it gives us such a great opportunity to analyse it in a safe space without any negative connotations. It is far more complex than that.

> I don't want any athlete to look back and regret all their success. But I did feel like that because I felt lost and I didn't know what to do. No one tells you this at the start of the journey.

Gail hit rock bottom in retirement. Entirely lost, devoid of confidence and with no idea of how to navigate the 'real' world, but she is a fighter and a grafter, and step by step has dragged herself forward.

> It was when I was doing some school talks with a Sky Sports scheme that I was working on. I was going to schools and talking to kids that actually hated sport, and we had to break down the aspects of sport, and one of them was knowing your support network, and it hit me: 'Maybe you should practise what you preach, Gail!' It hit me that I couldn't do this on my own, I needed a support network. I needed to call people. I'm stubborn and have always thought of myself as mentally tough, [someone] who can deal with everything on my own, but I had to face up to the fact that I couldn't do this like that. I started to put random messages out there asking people about work opportunities then slowly I just got this list of different people, random people, that could help me. I started getting enthusiastic again. Not everything worked but I found some new enthusiasm by reaching out. It was amazing.

It's clear that Gail has been and is still on a personal journey through retirement, and I wanted to know how she feels now about it all. How does she feel about that person from her past known as 'Gail Emms, the Olympic badminton player'?

It's still there. I think it always will be. It's like a bungee rope to my heart. This is the best way of describing it. I'm always in two minds whether to cut the cord. I've got two options, right? And for some people, they'll just cut the cord, move on to do something completely different. That's it, they've gone. For me, I can't do it and I don't want to do it. My cord is a bungee and most days I'm quite well away from it. I'm good, I'm fine. There will be things that literally just call me back. And I allow it because I think for me, my personality, the way I am, I'm okay with it. It will happen. There'll be days where I'll struggle because I'm quite an emotive person. I have to get the emotion out and then my head processes it. If I don't get the emotion out, then it's not good. That's what I've learned. But the feelings can come from anywhere. I've been working a lot in hospitality – I've been hosting or helping out as a waitress, and I did it at the Grand Prix recently and this woman I was serving champagne to said, 'Aren't you that badminton player? What are you doing this for?' But I'm okay with that now. I'll get those comments but you know what? I have to let it go, process it – I've got bills pay. I've got two kids, I'm a single mum. I also love hospitality. I get a lot of energy from it. In the past that comment would have broken me and I would have had to walk out and

I probably wouldn't have been able to go back in. It still hurts, but it's ok now.

As I write this out, it reminds me of a quote used by Donna VanLiere:

Grief never ends… But it changes. It's a passage, not a place to stay. Grief is not a sign of weakness, nor a lack of faith. It is the price of love.

Gail's experience of retirement has been heartbreak. Heartbreak of a love that we will talk about more in the next chapter. As the quote says, grieving is a long process and maybe it actually never ends. What is clear though is that retirement has forced Gail to find out who she really is because, as she said, 'I was lost.'

I don't feel happy and I don't feel sadness about my badminton career now. I feel acceptance. Maybe contentment, but I don't go, 'Oh my God, that's amazing.' I just feel it's part of my journey. I still think I've got lots more in my life that I want to do and I just think it was just one of my stepping stones, which is a little bit sad. The Athens Olympics final should have been one of the best days in my life but I don't feel overly happy or proud about it, just acceptance and contentment.

Although Gail doesn't feel sad about badminton anymore, her neutral feelings towards the sport makes me feel sad. It shouldn't be that way and something went very wrong.

Chapter 8

Gail Emms (Part 2)

When I hear the word 'ego' brought into a conversation, I always seem to envisage it as having a negative connotation, and I'm not exactly sure why that is. Maybe it is because I have heard phrases like 'his/her ego is out of control' or 'he/she has a massive ego' used as a criticism of people. Maybe it is because I have seen the respect given to, what appear to be, the humblest of sportspeople out there, such as Roger Federer. We seem to have enormous admiration for someone who can achieve greatness while still appearing grounded. We call it 'refreshing' and in contrast to someone displaying a big ego – or at least that's my perception of it. I wonder if we, or certainly I, have lost a real understanding of the role that ego plays in elite sportspeople, and particularly in the context of the challenges that they face in retirement. My conversation with Gail Emms was genuinely eye-opening. Her honesty and emotion provided me with powerful lessons that made me rethink my understanding around all of this.

When I came away from my chat with Gail, I began researching recent books and articles on ego. I wanted to dig deeper into where my perspective had come from and whether this aligned with other viewpoints out there. What I found was that the vast majority of recent narrative on ego was that it was destructive to someone. I found a book by Ryan Holiday called *Ego is the*

Enemy. The book provides an argument for why ego hurts us. In the book, Holiday writes:

> The ego we see most commonly goes by a more casual definition: an unhealthy belief in our own importance. Arrogance. Self-centred ambition... It's that petulant child inside every person, the one that chooses getting his or her way over anything or anyone else. The need to be better than, more than, recognized for, far past any reasonable utility – that's ego. It's the sense of superiority and certainty that exceeds the bounds of confidence and talent.

I found this paragraph absolutely fascinating within the context of my chat with Gail. Holiday is writing all of this in a negative context of why he believes ego doesn't help someone, but take for a minute the 7-year-old Gail Emms playing in an under-11s badminton tournament.

> I've got memories of when I was 7 years old and playing in an under-11s tournament and I got to the final. I remember all the other girls going, 'Wow, who is this girl?' It was more about that for me – very much about the adulation.

To this day, over 35 years later, Gail vividly remembers that powerful feeling. Now, a 7-year-old doesn't have any sort of understanding of what an ego is, nor could they be accused of having an 'out-of-control ego'; she was just a child. At that young age Gail had already fallen in love with winning and receiving the adulation from it – there was nothing wrong with that. And,

Matthew Hoggard appealing for a wicket in the 2005 Ashes at the Brit Oval. (*Alamy*)

Matthew Hoggard and Andrew Strauss walk off the pitch after the final day's play of a warm-up game against a CCI President's XI at the Brabourne Stadium in Mumbai, February 2006, ahead of the Test series against India. (*Flickr*)

Paul Walsh being tracked by Everton's John Bailey. (*Alamy*)

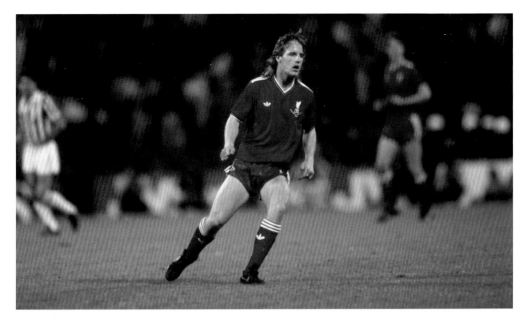

Walsh playing in Liverpool's European Cup Final against Juventus. (*Alamy*)

Walsh in his Manchester City days. (*Alamy*)

Gail Emms (L) returning a shot while her partner Nathan Robertson watches during their match against Japan's Shuichi Nakao and Aki Akao in the first round of the All England Open Badminton Championships, 2006. (*Alamy*)

Gail Emms and Nathan Robertson hold their silver medals from the mixed doubles badminton championship at the 2004 Olympic Games in Athens. The pair lost the gold medal to China's Zhang Jun and Gao Ling. (*Alamy*)

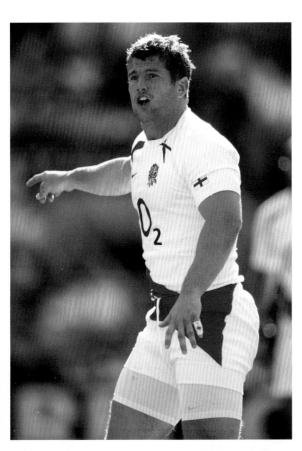

Tom May playing for England at Twickenham in 2009. (*Alamy*)

Tom May charges forward for Newcastle Falcons in a Premiership match against Bath. (*Alamy*)

Johnny Nelson gives Carl Thompson the hard stare after a press conference ahead of their WBO Cruiserweight Championship fight. (*Alamy*)

Johnny lands a punch on challenger George Arias, of Brazil, during their WBO Cruiserweight Championship boxing match in London's Bethnal Green. (*Alamy*)

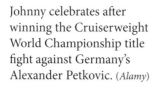

Johnny celebrates after winning the Cruiserweight World Championship title fight against Germany's Alexander Petkovic. (*Alamy*)

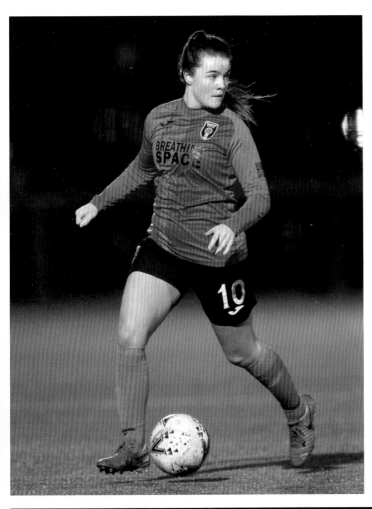

Glasgow City's Clare Shine during the UEFA Women's Champions League round of 16 second leg match. (*Alamy*)

Keeping wicket for Derbyshire in a Division Two County Championship match against Surrey at the Kia Oval. (*Alamy*)

Holding the pose in a Division One County Championship match between Lancashire and Essex at Chelmsford. (*Alamy*)

look back at the last line of Holiday's paragraph: 'It's the sense of superiority and certainty that exceeds the bounds of confidence and talent.' Well… DAMN RIGHT! The fact that the ego can exceed talent is exactly what can make someone become a history maker like Gail Emms. By Gail's own admission, she wasn't a particularly naturally talented badminton player, nothing like Nathan Robertson. Yet, her ego as a young and adult elite badminton player was an extremely powerful force in her doing so well. It was going to push her forward beyond her own natural ability. She was going to smash through brick walls when others gave up because she craved that feeling of adulation and status that winning gave her. There was nothing negative about that. It is not the same as any negative classification of ego. In fact, quite the opposite. In this context it is how ego can be enormously positive for an elite athlete. It's directed at the most intense feelings of wanting to win and then wanting the status for doing so. It is a great example of how we can misunderstand what ego can really do for someone. In my opinion, ego and status played fundamental roles in Gail's huge success in her sport, but also with her difficulties in retirement. But – and it is a big 'but' – don't for a minute think this was a superficial thing, like she was upset that people didn't recognise her in the street anymore; this was something far deeper. This was a heartbreaking loss for her of huge proportions. This was a lost love that she has had to grieve over a number of years, and maybe still is from time to time. Let me explain more.

From the age of 3 or 4, Gail wanted to be the best at badminton. She wasn't necessarily in love with the sport but she fell deeply in love with winning. She fell in love with what winning meant for her – adulation, status and respect. As she won more, she wanted more, her ego craved more. It is what kept driving her forward whenever there was an obstacle in her way during her career. And we must remember that Gail's journey within badminton was very much how I described the 'Road to Utopia' in an earlier chapter. Her whole life was pointing towards the Olympic dream. While other teenage girls were doing normal teenage things, Gail was focused on her sporting dreams. Years and years of sacrifice being driven by an intense desire to win, and importantly, be recognised for it. The Olympics was the holy grail for this journey. By the time Gail reached the Athens Olympics in 2004, she was 27 years old – two decades after she had fallen in love with the adulation she had received at that under-11s badminton tournament. There had been twenty years of build-up to this... the highest possible moment in sport... the Olympic Games. And then, guess what? They did it. They made history. They might not have won gold but Gail Emms and Nathan Robertson achieved something within their sport that no one had ever done before in Great Britain. It was incredibly special; they were incredibly special. And what followed was what Gail had always worked for – recognition. Parties and TV appearances followed where Gail could let go and enjoy everything she had ever worked for. It was all part of chasing and succeeding at the Olympic dream. Gail was in love with the position that she had finally achieved. Like she said, '"Hi, I'm Gail, I'm an Olympic badminton player"; people don't realise how much those words meant to me for status.'

Once the partying had subsided after Athens, Gail got back on the horse of the Olympic dream and this time headed towards the 2008 Beijing Games. In all honesty, when we consider everything we are talking about in this chapter, what choice did she have? Nothing in life was going to match what happened in Athens so the only thing to do was go again. Get back on the 'Road to Utopia'. Gail was in love with what she had achieved, what she could still achieve and who she was as a result. Again, there was absolutely nothing wrong with that. In fact, there was an immense amount of empowerment within that and it was what keeps many elite athletes relentless in their pursuit of further success. But the question is, where was this all heading? Where does this go when the playing days have to come to an end? You see, whether Gail continued after Beijing or not, she would have had to retire eventually or just not been selected. But then what? The 'Road to Utopia', the Olympic Dream, the years of sacrifice, 'Gail Emms – the Olympic badminton player'... where does that all go? The truth is that it just simply... stops. It dies. But as Gail said, 'No one tells you that.' No one tells you at the start of the Olympic dream that once you get to the other side then you might just have your heart broken into a million pieces regardless of what success you have ever achieved. You see, the loss that Gail has felt so intensely is the loss of... her – 'Gail Emms, the Olympic badminton player'. She loved the feeling of winning but more importantly, she was deeply in love with what that made her. It solidified her feelings of self-worth, purpose and status. Yet, no one ever warned her during her playing career that she was becoming more and more defined as a person by her badminton success, not by who she really was. While you're a 'robot badminton player' that's fine because you are there to win medals and secure funding for the future of the sport, and it is satisfying your ego that has helped you become the success you are. It's actually a marriage of convenience for all parties, except for when the athlete has to retire. The sport spits you out and looks for a younger version, while the athlete is left in ruins wondering who the hell they are. They realise that the person they thought they were doesn't exist anymore.

This realisation took time for Gail, though, because quite literally, no one told her about it, and how was she to know when she had been conditioned in a particular 'Olympic' way for the best part of thirty years? There is not a switch someone can just turn off and on. Gail walked into normal life, trying to find her way, unaware that the person and persona that she thought she was didn't exist anymore. And this wasn't about being back at the bottom of the pile of anything. As she said, 'Don't get me wrong, I'm used to starting back at the bottom and I'm working my way up.' Gail had no issue with working her way back up from whatever. The truth is that anyone who knows her will testify that she is one of life's grafters. The issue was more centred on not knowing how she fitted into normal life. The rules seemed to be different – the ways people interacted with her were different, she didn't know where on the ladder she sat and she didn't know what she needed to do to make progress. This is, of course, tapping into how elite sportspeople love structure within their lives and Gail suddenly felt it vanishing. Sportspeople love knowing what the situation is and what they need to improve – that is exactly why they are exceptional in difficult situations. The crapness of a situation is never something they dwell on because they immediately move into trying to solve it – out of the problem and into the solution. Yet, in normal life, there appeared to be no structure for this for Gail. Not getting a job but then not receiving any feedback as to why is the equivalent of losing a match and your coach not explaining to you what went wrong. It is completely foreign to an elite sportsperson. They can take hard feedback because ultimately, they want to improve as quickly as possible. Nonetheless, in my opinion, Gail's challenges with the lack of structure were all underpinned because she was suffering a huge crisis of who she actually was.

If your entire life and persona has been built around sporting success and then there is no sporting success to hook that onto then what do you do? Ultimately, you have to let go of the past, discover who you are today and then move forward, but that is tough and takes a lot of time. It is even tougher doing it as an adult in your thirties and, for instance, being a new mum. Everything would feel uncertain and 'abnormal' to you but the world itself would just want you to fit into 'normal'. Nobody would understand why you felt sad, confused or even angry about what life looked like now. And before you are even able to move forward, you have to let go of the person you were before, but what if that person was exactly what you had always dreamed of being? What if you didn't want to let go of them? Then it becomes an incredibly painful process and eventually, a grieving one. For Gail, she needed to grieve the person she had worked so hard to be and loved being so much. This isn't a narcissistic thing, more a heart-wrenching lost love thing. Gail's story is a classic tale of how the Olympic dream that is presented to young athletes has been so fundamentally flawed in the past, and possibly even now. Nothing should have dissuaded Gail from working as hard as she did or sacrificing as much as she did to the sport. Without it she would have been found out and not achieved what she did. But there wasn't any real duty of care taken over what type of person was being cultivated by British Badminton and UK Sport. Gail's challenges in retirement should have been of no surprise to anyone, most of all her, because she should have been warned. She should have received time and care from people within UK Sport to explain to her how life would change in retirement and how she might find that extremely difficult. Instead, she was thrust off the conveyor belt, while they were busy searching for the next Gail Emms, and left to work it all out for herself.

I think any sports fan would agree that something cannot be right if one of our sporting heroes or heroines, such as Gail, looks back on their sport with any sort of resentment or anger. Something has badly failed in that instance. In Gail's case, what made her a history maker in badminton also left her in retirement sobbing on the sofa, wondering whether any of it was worth it. The impact of ego and status can be enormously powerful for an elite sportsperson but it needs to be understood because in retirement it can also be very destructive as the fundamentals of their life shift entirely.

I loved speaking to Gail. Her raw emotion was one of the things that inspired me to write this book and why I want to do justice to her experience in writing about it. She made me rethink a lot of perspectives I already had and gave me a bigger perspective on the challenges athletes face in retirement. Powerful lessons are there to be learned from Gail's story.

Chapter 9

Tom May (Part 1)

Tom May's career record in professional rugby might well become a thing of the past.

Tom retired at the age of 37 having made 380 top-flight appearances for Newcastle Falcons, Toulon, Northampton Saints and London Welsh, as well as gaining two full England caps. His career spanned nearly twenty years. In a time when retirement ages from professional rugby are getting younger by the minute due to the brutal physical nature of the sport, Tom's record is incredibly impressive. Yet his record is also a reflection of who he is as a person and was as a professional sportsman. For full transparency, I know Tom very well. During the final years of his rugby career, he did some consultancy work for my talent management business, and without meaning to embarrass him, he is one of life's good blokes – a hard worker who lives by important values of trust and honesty. He was a model professional rugby player and if you were going to war, you'd want him right by your side.

I was always prepared to work hard because I knew I wasn't going to be the quickest, fastest, strongest, or whatever, but I knew I could graft harder than anyone else. I was lucky with injuries, but also I worked hard for twenty years and I looked after myself. I was always good at getting the boring stuff done in training and recovery, and that actually gets you a long way.

Tom was meticulous as a professional rugby player – organised and thorough, who left no stone unturned. So, it shouldn't surprise you that is how he also prepared for retirement. He was as pro-active about it as any professional sportsperson that I have ever met.

My dad was always like, 'What are you going to do if you break your leg?' And I was like, 'Please Dad, just let me enjoy this moment!' But actually, looking back, my dad drilling into me about taking care of things away from rugby helped in ways I don't think he was meaning to. In nineteen years, I only had one year where I didn't do anything off the field, and it was probably the year I played the worst. Because I was always doing something off the field, rugby became a much more simplified version of itself, less of a 'job'.

When it came to training or match time, I had this feeling that I had finished my work and could have fun having a run around. I think it provided me with quite a bit of balance and helped me be a more rounded person. I was always interested in what sponsors were up to. When I met them they were always more interested in what professional rugby was like but I wanted to know how they set their business up and what made it so good. Whether I was doing courses or setting up new businesses, I was always trying something.

It's safe to say that Tom had an immediate outlook on rugby, and what was beyond it, that would be considered 'healthy' when approaching retirement. He wasn't ever in denial that he would need to find a life beyond rugby. As I've already mentioned, I have had personal experience of working with Tom while he was still playing rugby, and he was always eager to learn more about the business world and what made it tick. Despite a hugely impressive career, it also never felt like he defined himself by his rugby. In these scenarios, I sometimes wonder if it is because the sportsperson in question might have not always been destined for stardom and therefore have this grounding to them. They've likely had to work harder than most to achieve what they have and tend to have a broader outlook on life. But I'm not sure this applies to Tom and it was more to do with the influence that his parents had on him. His secondary schooling was at Tonbridge School in Kent, where he had already been identified as a talent.

No one really said it directly, but I could tell that I was rated. My housemaster at school used to play for Harlequins and he used to get me in and talk to me about my game. He basically let me do what I wanted if it was based around rugby. And I knew I was getting given slightly more leeway than my mates. And actually, the First XV coach at school, a man called Graham Gales, I think he used to treat me the same way. Now, looking back, I was getting probably looked after slightly better.

So, in the context of this book, Tom was very different to most others – he was preparing for retirement almost all his career.

He was well aware that there was life beyond rugby and that he would need to improve himself to be ready for it. He was ready to try new things and to work as hard as he could. And all of this was despite him having an outstanding pathway throughout his rugby career from school all the way to the full England side. So, you would imagine that he had an easy or easier transition into retirement?

> Everyone used to say to me, 'You'll be all right because you've been preparing for retirement for forever,' but I reckon it took me three years to find my feet. To start with I was trying to find something to replace the weekend. I suddenly realised that Friday nights were amazing and I'd go out, but when I went out, I *really* went out. Yes, I was still training, but I realised that there was no release at the weekend when I played rugby, where I could build up all that training, pent-up aggression, whatever it might be, and let it all out on the Saturday. Whereas I was sort of building, building and building and then like, 'Shit, where am I going to take this?' Which was difficult. I did some stupid stuff at the time. Not really bad stuff, but I wouldn't want to behave like that now.

I have always felt that professional rugby has similarities with the military forces, and I will add to this point within this chapter. There is an innate physicality to them both that prepares people for war – in rugby, that is the match at the weekend. There is a weekly cycle to it, which means the match is vital to let out all tension that's built up in training during the week. In simple terms, the match is the 'purpose'. So, without the match, what happens? Tom faced other huge challenges in retirement despite all the preparation he had put in.

> I got myself into a massive financial mess when I finished. I was in a hole and I wasn't great at talking about it. In the end I knew that I needed to go and see my dad about it, which felt like a nightmare for me. Not because he's my dad but because I had to go to him asking for help. It was a pride thing but there's no other way out here. I had no other option; it was a rock bottom. But, I sat down and chatted to him and he was actually amazing. He didn't judge me, he just wanted to work out how we sorted it.

For someone seemingly so prepared for retirement, how had this happened? Well, a divorce and living in London certainly didn't help, but it was also a sharp introduction to a working life outside of rugby.

> Having been tied to one thing forever, in rugby, I didn't want to be tied to one thing in retirement, so I was trying to do consultancy work with lots of different companies, but I learned some very harsh lessons in the process. My sister has always told me that I land on my feet, but actually, I definitely didn't land on my feet after leaving rugby. The real tough times that other people have experienced through their lives, I got them all in one go in retirement. And it's pretty difficult to have that level of intensity of just constant crap all the time, to keep moving. It's difficult.

I can understand this, though. I have been similar since my cricket career. I have always found the thought of doing just one thing for work in retirement really difficult to get my head around. Nothing is ever going to match playing professional sport but I guess if you can have multiple things challenging you then it feels a bit more exciting.

I think initially I was like, 'Oh, wow, this is awesome. I've got so much freedom. No one's telling me what to do. I don't feel like I have to do something.' I went into business development for various different companies and set out as a consultant. I was doing a fair bit of media but unfortunately, big media companies don't pay quickly. It was a completely different world to work in. I was used to it being payday and money was in my account. But the biggest lesson I learned was when I got my first big role. It was good money, I didn't have to do it all day, every day. And then out of nowhere, my contract just got pulled after three months. The contract had a three-month clause in it, meaning he owed me three months of money, but he knew I wasn't going to be able to do anything about it. I quickly realised that when you're in a changing room with thirty blokes, you might have thirty different opinions, but you're all pushing in one direction. Importantly, we trust each other. There's a code of trust. Suddenly, in the corporate world, different opinions also meant different agendas going on. But because of rugby, my first instinct is still to trust people. Honesty is a huge part of what we did. You've got to be honest with yourself and teammates, it's how it works. But as Becky, my wife, will say to me now – it's different; you've got to be careful about people and don't back someone to the hilt until you really know them.

This brings us back to my comparison of rugby and the military forces, but I believe it can extend to other sports. In professional sport, you go to battle with your teammates and for that to function well, there needs to exist a code between you. That will be a code of behaviour of how you treat and respect each other. That code is sacrosanct in high-performing teams and if you need an example, look no further than the New Zealand rugby team, the All Blacks. Values like trust, respect and honesty are pivotal. This was part of who Tom was because rugby had been woven into his life from such a young age. He was 'from' rugby.

I was a bit of a 'Sport Billy'. Given any opportunity, I'd be doing something to do with sport. But even before rugby turned professional, when I was growing up, I was saying to my parents that I wanted to be a rugby player. One of my heroes growing up was Rob Andrew, and I used to love watching him. And my dad played Old Boys rugby and I spent hours on Saturdays just kicking balls over posts while my mum and dad were having a few drinks in the bar. I'd be outside and it was going dark, still kicking balls. I loved that chance to just go out there and practise. And games on television, I'd watch it all. And I loved the physicality of rugby. I used to have rugby birthday parties, so all my mates that weren't into rugby would turn up and they'd be like, 'What the hell is this?' Some of them didn't want to get muddy, but I would be head to toe in mud.

Tom fell in love with rugby and being a rugby player almost immediately. He loved the nature of the sport and everything it brought with it, and that included the values that he saw in it – whether that was from watching his heroes on television or his dad play for the Old Boys. I would hazard a guess that Tom also loved being part of a team working towards a common cause – something with honour? This felt evident when I asked him where he most liked playing his rugby.

> I think Northampton and Toulon, it was being central to a team that was central to a town or a city. I loved being a big part of a town's pride where they live and breathe rugby. So having had the opportunity to experience that with those two teams was great. It gave me a serious purpose to what I was doing because otherwise I think you can drift.

It also explained to me why Tom had such longevity in the sport. He genuinely loved playing rugby and being part of the sport. Now, that might sound obvious, but it's really not. When some professional sportspeople approach the end of their careers, they start tiring of the actual matches – they are 'done'. I was very much in that case with cricket. But not Tom; he just wanted to play for as long as he could.

> One of the main reasons I moved to London Welsh at the end of my career was because I wanted to play. I had

a chance to go to Leicester but I didn't want to sit there on the bench. I also wanted to be in London to activate some connections but I loved playing in the Premiership at 37 years old. It probably doesn't sound right but we were getting battered, and I loved it because I was just like, 'Right, this is my last hurrah and I'm going to give it everything.' And I didn't take a backwards step from anyone. I was trying to set an example for the young lads, because I also knew that when it was done, I was out. But... even though my body was hanging off and I'd finished with London Welsh, I went back down south and started playing club rugby for Sevenoaks!

By the time Tom finished playing professional rugby his roots in the sport were, as expected, very deep and this was bound to have an impact on how he found life in retirement. Even the physical fitness required to be a rugby player was something really important to him after his playing days had finished.

Yeah, weirdly, I always loved pre-season, when you get a chance to get fit, get strong and really look after yourself for a bit. But even to this day, I get up at twenty to six every morning, I'm at the gym waiting for it to open at six, do my training, out by five to seven and back home for ten to seven for breakfast with the kids. It's part of my day. If I don't do it, I know I'm either going to be a grumpy bastard or not be the person I want to be. One thing that I have always had structure and control of is my training. I've got control over how much I push myself. Because, there's so many different things going on in a business environment in comparison to sport. Yeah, there's a lot of things going on in sport, but generally they're all moving in one direction for a particular reason. There's just far too many different moving parts in business but I can feel in control with my training, whether I'm running or whatever I'm doing.

Control and structure seem understandably important to Tom, as they have been with all the other athletes that I have spoken to.

In sport, if you have lost then you know that you need to get better at this or you need to do that. There's an element of that in the business world, but it's different. If I didn't get picked and if I'm given a reason, I'll go and fix that. Well, that doesn't happen in the business world. It just doesn't happen the way that it happens in sport. And so I think that's something that sportspeople have to get used to – feedback doesn't come. And if it does come, it probably comes in a format that either you don't understand or it's not structured the way that you would expect it to be. There's no 'just go and do A, B, and C, and you'll be fine'.

Tom has definitely come out the other side of his journey in retirement. As we chat, he's only a few weeks away from getting married and is happy and healthy. He's settled in his working life and seems content. I asked him what he would tell a younger Tom May who was getting ready for retirement.

The world is different so be prepared. Be prepared by not just having a 'plan', but by going out and speaking to people. Go and follow people around. Get an understanding of what a workplace looks and feels like. And, yeah, you're going to be at a point in time in your life, in your thirties if you're lucky, where you're going to have to swallow your pride and ask some fucking stupid questions that the little spotty teenager on an intern placement already knows the answer to. When I finished rugby, I didn't know whether it was corporate people trying to get one up on this sportsman coming in or they were just talking a language I didn't understand, but there was no way I could understand what they were saying – and that's alright, but ask questions. It also depends who you are and if you're in the 1 per cent like a John Terry, then you can just work on your golf, but if you're like 99 per cent of other professional sportspeople coming into retirement then money is going to have a big impact on how your transition will be. No one really talks about it because it's money but it plays a big role in how much time you have available. But this biggest thing is the reinvention, letting go of the old you. Not the old you, but the status of the old you. In my case, a rugby player, but I'm not that anymore. I'm just a fucking bloke. Tell yourself, 'That's gone, mate. Now, what's the next step?' That's difficult when you have to drop the guillotine quickly on that, but that might be required. Life moves forward and you have to keep moving forward. The pace at which you can do this is the

issue that some sportspeople face. If you can't let go of
it, your problems are going to keep coming at you.

The final point that Tom made here about the 'letting go'
seems enormously important and something we will come back
to. Tom's experience was of someone who was in many ways
perfectly prepared for retirement – he ticked so many boxes –
but it wasn't as simple as that for him. He experienced some
extremely tough times, which have taken him years to work
through.

As we move into the next chapter, I want you to ask yourself
this question: Can someone truly be prepared for what's next if
it is completely different to how they have been conditioned for
most of their life?

Chapter 10

Tom May (Part 2)

T here is a great deal of honour in rugby.

Immensely strong men and women battle it out on the field in the hardest of physical battles and yet simultaneously and wholeheartedly respect each other and the laws of the game. You only have to watch a tiny referee reprimanding two enormous players like naughty school kids and them nodding in apology to understand this. It is why rugby players have the biggest of eye rolls when they see some of the pathetic antics that happen in professional football. There is also fundamental honour within the internal dynamics of a rugby team. Physically they have to prepare themselves for a war and then they have to fight that war together. When they share those moments, they get to see the depth of their courage in one another and it bonds them. It bonds them beyond a superficial liking of each other; it bonds them as teammates, as warriors standing side by side ready to protect and support each other. A fundamental trust is borne between them. This is the world that Tom May grew up in and then had nearly twenty years in as a professional rugby player. That is how he thought the world worked.

Tom was a ten-out-of-ten professional rugby player and his career record speaks volumes to back that up. He was the same in approaching retirement. Hard work, preparation and plans were all there. As Tom said, 'Everyone used to say to me, "You'll be all right because you've been preparing for retirement for forever.'" In nineteen years of professional rugby, he only had one year in which he didn't do something outside of rugby. He knew that he needed to appreciate the world outside of rugby and took positive action to do this. And yet, he still reached a massive rock bottom in retirement. Financial ruin was a real possibility for him. This brings me back to the point that I have made earlier in the book that I believe there is some myth in the belief that if you prepare well for retirement from professional sport, all will be fine. It is far more complex than that. We have to understand the conditioning of the sportsperson to get to the bottom of this rather than look at how many courses they have put themselves on. Tom walked into a business world he was seemingly prepared for but was actually completely unprepared for – someone had changed the rules of life and not told him. For the vast majority of Tom's life, he had operated under a code that rugby had taught him – a bunker mentality. Everyone is in this together whether we like each other or not, so let's work as a team and move forward. But then... BANG... along came corporate life, and it wasn't like that. People didn't always behave with honour and you couldn't always trust someone who was meant to be in your team. There seemed to be a million moving parts in the corporate world with too many competing agendas. You may be working for the same company, you might even be working for the same team within a department of the same company, but self-interest could run riot. The common goal of hitting a profit target feels nothing like winning a hard rugby match with fourteen teammates. One feels tangible and one feels like a corporate soundbite. Winning two more points will move your team up the Premiership table; making higher profits for your company will mean... exactly what? And within all this, people are trying to climb the corporate ladder from varying spots that they are starting from. Yes, people are working together but at the same time they have a close eye on their individual progression within the office or for their company – hardly like trusting your teammate to protect you when your body is on the line in a match. If this type of environment went against your newly found values it would sting a bit, but now imagine that those things go against the fundamental way you have lived your life for thirty years – it would seem like an earthquake.

If you are not convinced on how jarring this would be for someone like Tom, remember how long it took him to find some stability in retirement – three years. And Tom is one of the most switched-on, earnest and hardworking ex-athletes out there. It is why in the previous chapter, I wanted to bring comparison between professional rugby and the military services. I believe there is a lot of similarity and I expect ex-military personnel walking into 'normal' life would find it equally as difficult. The fact that the rules of life seem to have changed is one thing but harder is that no one has prepared them for it. The reason for this is you can't un-condition someone while you need them to be conditioning themselves in the opposite way in order to perform their jobs within sport or the military. For example, the fundamentals of trust, commitment, purpose and respect are paramount to a team's success on a rugby field, so why would you try to caution a player during their playing days on those in order to prepare them for the outside world? You just wouldn't. Someone can prepare as much as they like but that reality is going to hit them in a hard way in retirement.

The physical aspect for both rugby and the military is also an important point for us to look at within this. The physical conditioning of rugby players is a huge part of their lives. You can't put your body on the line every single weekend and not want to be as prepared for that as you can be. If you're not willing to do that then you will be out of the game at the highest level very quickly. I would expect the same to apply to people in the military. What is on the line for both of them is very significant, although granted, it is much more serious for the military. That level of physical conditioning can't be understated. We have to appreciate the build-up to the weekend, or the 'battle'. The physical anticipation to this is huge – there will be adrenaline, excitement and even a bit of fear. The match itself is a massive release for them. So, the cycle of physical training and then match-day release is integral within a rugby player's mentality and that can't be switched off easily. That's why it didn't surprise me when Tom talked about how he tried to find something to replace the weekends at the start of retirement, and that caused problems for him. He had been conditioned for all his rugby playing days to prepare extremely hard for the release at the weekends, and suddenly it wasn't there. There will come a time when all ex-athletes who are still training hard will ask themselves, 'What am I actually preparing for?' There is no war at the weekend anymore; there is no release of all this pent-up tension; there is no purpose anymore. That void can be a dangerous spot to be in as an ex-professional sportsperson because they won't feel comfortable in it, and will look for a release in another way. It is why addiction issues in retirement are so prevalent.

Nonetheless, the physical side that rugby taught Tom is something that he has eventually been able to channel in a constructive way. Remember what he said about his training in retirement:

One thing that I have always had structure and control of is my training. I've got control over how much I push myself.

Whether they know it or not, professional sportspeople crave structure to their life and while they are playing, it is there in abundance. Physical training adds another layer on to this for rugby players. It is their 'time' to feel some control in their world and that is crucial for them. During a time in his life in which he felt like so much was suddenly out of control, Tom's training was an anchor that he could attach to and this has continued to this day. His daily routine of being in the gym as soon as it opens at six in the morning has become a necessity for him in order to feel like he can be the best possible dad, husband and person in life. Whether that has been a conscious thing or not, that is where he has found a different purpose to his training rather than it being about the weekend 'release'.

Without finding this change in the reason or purpose for the physical training that they so enjoy, an ex-professional sportsperson will really struggle. It will feel like a constant conflict in their mind – they want to do it but they don't really know why. They could even go through periods of doing no training and eventually hate themselves for it because that physical strength is so conditioned into their mindset.

There is definitely no ego to Tom, certainly in any negative sense. He's always been a very affable and humble person to be around. The egocentric side to the status of being a professional rugby player just didn't seem to ever be a thing for him, especially towards the end of his sports career. However, 'status' is a more complicated concept than we might think. Tom didn't mind not being a professional rugby player any more as a job per se but, and this is crucial, there was an old version of him that lived in that status that he has had to learn to let go of. That version of him was the one that had been conditioned to 'being' a professional rugby player – living life under the rules that the game had taught him, and having expectations based on what the game had shown him. It is this version of Tom that initially drowned in retirement, and it was for all the reasons that we have discussed in this chapter. I believe that Tom is pragmatic by nature but he had to learn the hard way that life in retirement was very different. Importantly, he had to learn that he would need to adjust to that rather than life adjusting to him.

Sadly, many professional sportspeople find this extremely difficult. They loved their old life, status and way of living, and don't want to accept that it needs to change. As Tom explained, this is ok if you're in the top 1 per cent of professional sportspeople who never have to work again or can at least enjoy some financial freedom in retirement, but that is only for a very few. For the vast majority, they need to work again immediately, and that requires them adjusting to life outside of professional sport very quickly. If they don't, they will feel the pain of that. And if they persist with not adjusting then that pain will keep hitting them. But take a minute to consider this further – if for all of your adult life you have just needed to be yourself and show off your natural abilities as a sportsperson to generate attention and money, then how do you easily let go of it? It has worked all their life up until retirement, so why the change? Does it mean someone having to be less of the person they think they are? That's a complicated sentence to write, let alone to understand! But Tom's experience shows us that he did need to un-learn or un-condition himself from the old Tom May that lived in rugby, and in some senses maybe his humility helped this process happen faster than it could have happened. Later in this book I will talk about my own personal experiences on this particular aspect because I think it is absolutely crucial to our understanding of why athletes struggle or thrive in retirement and the pace at which they can do both.

I felt that Tom was an important person for me to include in this book because he cannot be categorised as someone who was in denial about retirement coming one day. In fact, he was the exact opposite, but he still had his serious struggles. There is a great deal for us to learn from Tom's experiences and they challenge some of the very basic thinking around professional sport that tells athletes that they just need to gain an extra qualification or two in order to prepare for the outside world. There are more layers to this whole thing that need to be peeled back in order to truly understand it.

But, just maybe, for the athlete themselves, some of those lessons simply can't be learned until they are in the middle of the harsh reality of what retirement feels like.

Chapter 11

Johnny Nelson (Part 1)

Johnny Nelson's story is unique.

We live in a world obsessed with 'high performance'. If you don't believe me then just have look at how much content is out there on the subject at the moment for books, podcasts and documentaries – it is everywhere. We simply can't get enough of hearing about how one person or a team has become or can be 'the best of the best'. We are fascinated as to how our 'greats' have achieved what they have. And, why is that? Well, I think it's because we want to understand a sphere of performance that we don't feel we can get close to. We want to feel a little closer to the 'gods'.

Modern-day society has only heightened this obsession. Social media has created a culture of wanting everything NOW, including answers to any questions we may have. We want every bit of information we can possibly get in as few clicks as possible. So, as a new footballer thrives in the Premier League, we frantically search online for the reasons why they have become so brilliant – we want the whole back story.

The truth is that we currently have one of two back stories behind every great sportsperson. The first is simple – they were born a genius, like a Diego Maradona or a Paul Gascoigne. They were simply blessed with extraordinary natural ability, which, even despite their ill-discipline, meant they were always going to be great. The second is that they were made into a genius

– from a very early age, maybe 3 or 4 years old, they were put on a path to be created into the best, like a Tiger Woods or a Serena Williams. They will have shown some natural ability as a child. But this story is much more about a process than instinct. At the moment, that's it for us, it can only be one of those two ways. Well, that's not entirely true. We are ok with having some sort of blend of the two, i.e. they were nearly born a great but then worked so hard that they became a great, e.g. Cristiano Ronaldo. If you really look at it, our understanding of high performance is pretty good when it comes to what happens in the sporting arena but our understanding of how that person got there is still fairly limited. The story of Johnny Nelson is a great example of this.

Make no mistake, Johnny is one of our boxing greats. He is currently the longest reigning world cruiserweight champion of all time, having held the WBO title from 1999 to 2005. Johnny defended the title against thirteen different fighters, more than any other cruiserweight in history, and holds a joint record of most consecutive cruiserweight title defences (along with Marco Huck). Those are career records not to be sniffed at on any level. Once Johnny reached the highest level, he was unbeatable, and it was only injury that stopped his career. That in itself is extremely rare. But then consider this, the same Johnny Nelson who put together this immense career record also said to me: 'I can honestly say that I was shit.'

Maybe false modesty or an impression of himself when he was just a kid? No, not at all. He felt this way when he was in his mid-twenties and he was already a British champion! You see, whatever back story we see in our greats of sport, we believe that along the way they must have built up a large amount of self-belief – confidence that pulls them through the tough moments.

It's why we often hear that elite sportspeople need an element of arrogance about them. Well, Johnny simply didn't have any of that. Zero! It is this single point that makes his story during his career and then into retirement so remarkable.

The thing is that I wasn't in love with the fight game. In fact, it was hate for boxing straight away as a kid. The only reason why I boxed in the first place was to make friends at the gym. You see, I loved going to school because I was with my mates but that was it. When I left school, I hadn't done any exams and had the reading and writing age of a 10-year-old. So, once I left school, my friends were going to work and I wasn't. I realised that I didn't have any friends anymore. My eldest brother, Bob, was my hero and I followed him everywhere and he used to go to the boxing club. But my brother understood, when he started boxing, that it wasn't a game, and I was a bit of a joker so, to start with, he wouldn't let me go to the club. Eventually, when I had left school, I finally got there, though, because I just felt like I needed to make some friends. But the downside of going to the boxing club was having to box! I didn't want to box, I just wanted to make mates. I definitely didn't want to be hit! I actually had fifteen amateur fights and only won three of them. I was terrible. I would just grab and hold to get through the fights and people would take the piss out of me and say, 'This kid's rubbish'. I didn't want to be there. I remember travelling on the bus to some of the amateur shows and the guys would be talking about knocking somebody out, how they're going to do it, and

I'd be shitting myself, thinking, 'Oh my God, what??
I can never do that. I'm not good enough for that.'

I just need to add context around this again – Johnny wasn't a
young kid at this point, he was a young adult. In our traditional
storytelling of what makes a great sportsperson, he was far too
behind everyone else at this point in time at that age. There
is literally nothing in what he describes that would make you,
or him, for that matter, believe that he would go on to be the
greatest cruiserweight boxer this country has ever produced. But
there was one man who changed this.

Brendan Ingle was a renowned boxing trainer who ran the
boxing club that Johnny went to with his brother to just 'make
some friends'. During Ingle's time at Wincobank Gym in
Sheffield, he coached and managed four world champions. They
were 'Prince' Naseem Hamed, Kell Brook, Junior Witter and…
Johnny Nelson.

I believe that I was supposed to meet Brendan Ingle,
a truly beautiful man. It was his mission then to turn
me from a boy into a man. It was his mission then to
talk me into a life in boxing. It was his mission then to
be patient enough for me to grow, mature and to fall in
love with boxing. But he told me I wouldn't fall in love
with boxing until I'm in my late twenties or thirties. To
me, at 15, that was very old. And I thought, I'm not
going to be boxing when I'm like, 25. He's mad! But he
understood the long process it would take for me to fall
in love with boxing. And he said, 'You're going to win,
lose, draw, but you're going to learn, and if you stick at

it, you'll be a world champion.' Now, I never in a million years believed I was going to be world champion. So this guy was like a nutty professor. He had a Walt Disney mentality, where he could see what could possibly be created, but everybody else around him thought, 'Never! He can't do that; you can never do it.' But he could see that in me. He said, 'If you just listen to me to get there, you'll be a world champion.'

When Johnny spoke about Brendan, it reminded me of the famous quote from Edmund Lee:

Surround yourself with the dreamers and the doers, the believers and thinkers, but most of all, surround yourself with those who see the greatness within you, even when you don't see it yourself.

Never could this have applied more than to the story of Johnny Nelson and Brendan Ingle.

The even more extraordinary part of Johnny's story is that despite him hating the sport, having a poor amateur career and having virtually no self-belief, he and Brendan got him to two world title fights – but this fact adds another layer to this whole thing. Johnny's first two world title fights were a disaster. It wasn't just that Johnny lost both, it was more the manner of the defeats. In January 1990, Johnny had his first world title fight against Puerto Rican Carlos de Leon at Sheffield's City Hall. It was his big night in front of a home crowd and maybe the night when everything Ingle had told him over the years would come true. But he froze and struggled to throw any meaningful punch combinations. He drew the bout, due to a lack of action, and the fans' reaction was terrible. He was ridiculed in Sheffield and called a coward. As he told me, he thought he was shit, and everyone else thought he was useless. Every doubt, every bit of hate towards the sport, and any hope of self-confidence was blown to pieces. To give you a feel of how bad it got, when Ingle came up with an idea to get the public behind their local hero, offering £750 for anyone who would spend the week sparring with him, a man dressed as Rambo turned up saying his wife had sent him 'to do' Johnny as they needed the money for a three-piece suite. It was horrific. The spiralling negativity pushed Johnny into depression but Ingle absolutely refused to give up on him, even if Johnny was ready to give up on himself.

The only reason why I kept going back was because of Brendan. He spent time with me, he spoke to me. I actually used to wish that I was one of his kids. His house was across the road from the gym. He had five kids, two daughters, three boys, and I see them all going through the house and I'd think, 'God, I wish I was one of those kids.' Not disrespecting my stepdad, not disrespecting my mum, but he taught me about life through the stories he told; he educated me in a way that I didn't realise I was being educated. He spoke to me about so many different things. He taught me how to think on my feet, he taught me how to understand human nature. And I was like a sponge listening. But I wasn't the only one. We all did, we all had the opportunity. Brendan was that father figure that we just gravitated towards because it wasn't just about training the body, it's about training the mind. You see, education isn't just about going to school and studying geography, maths, history and science. There's life skills but there weren't life teachers or coaches. Brendan was a life coach. That's what inspired me and so it was probably that I didn't want to let him down.

The effect Ingle had on Johnny really can't be overstated. His point-blank refusal to give up on him and his constant attention to develop him as a person and as a fighter was there for everyone to see. As Johnny said earlier, Ingle was 'on a mission'.

The second world title fight was two years later against James Warring, and again, Johnny lost, this time beaten on a unanimous decision. He was 25 years old, there was still absolutely nothing to suggest that Johnny would go on to do what he did. But Ingle kept giving him time and repeating this phrase to him over and over again: 'You're going to win, lose, draw, but you're going to learn, and if you stick at it, you'll be a world champion.' The bond Johnny must have felt between him and Ingle would have been something very special – like a father and son.

Remarkably, the persistence paid off as Johnny got himself a third world title fight in 1999. It really was last chance saloon for him when he got the opportunity to fight Carl Thompson in Derby. Thompson was a formidable opponent. He had just retired rock-hard Chris Eubank Sr with back-to-back defeats and went on to be the only man to beat David Haye at cruiserweight. Bearing in mind Johnny's history on the big occasion, there was a lot to feel nervous about if you were in his camp, but, incredibly, he did it and stopped Thompson in the fifth round and gloriously became WBO cruiserweight world champion. He wept in the ring with Ingle. Pure emotion flowed out of him.

> Brendan always had a saying: 'You haven't got the confidence to match your ability.' And there are many people in this world that are like that. They have the ability, but they don't have the belief, the confidence within themselves to execute that ability. So I don't know if it was something in my make-up, something how I spoke, something how I looked at stuff, something how I listened – I don't know why he gave me that time. I don't know why he gave me that patience and stuck with me. I don't know why he was the only one that defended me when everybody else was against me. I have no idea what he saw, but what I do know, he was right. And everything he said to me, with regards to my career, happened. Everything I achieved, even though nobody could see it, not even me, happened. And so it's not about manifestation, it's just about finding a way, it's about mindset. And Brendan made me realise that my mind was a blank canvas so I could be brainwashed in a good way.

If anyone looked back on Johnny's entire boxing history up to that moment when he beat Carl Thompson to become world champion, even the harshest cynic would have to admit that is a truly remarkable story. But even after the victory, questions must have existed. Maybe it was a fluke? Maybe Johnny wasn't up to that standard and would be quickly found out? Well, no. Call it his positive brainwashing or his vision, everything Ingle had told Johnny over the many years suddenly clicked and there was no looking back for him.

> I finally loved the sport, just like Brendan had told me. And when I knew I was in love with it, I knew I would never lose again.

And sure enough, Johnny never lost again. He was only forced into retirement through a serious knee injury sustained in the build-up to his incredible fourteenth defence of his world title versus Enzo Maccarinelli in 2006. Johnny's boxing journey from notoriety for the wrong reasons to notoriety for great reasons was over. He would forever be remembered as one of our boxing greats who travelled a truly unique pathway to get there.

So, what next for Johnny? How does such an extraordinary bond between coach and fighter transition into retirement? How does a boy who became a man through the tutelage of Brendan Ingle and boxing move on to something else?

> I remember, I was doing an interview a couple days before I retired, and the interviewer said to me, 'What will you miss most about the gym?' I'd never thought about that up till then. And I started to cry because that realisation hit me. I thought, 'Shit, I'm gonna miss Brendan.' I'd miss seeing him every day and miss being in the gym with the boys, my family. So all of a sudden it started to dawn on me like a rain cloud in the distance, thinking, 'Shit!' It was that one question that made me worry, that made me start to think about tomorrow and what it would feel like. You see, I was always a mummy's

boy. I love the stability of family. Even though there were seven kids in my whole household with four different fathers, we were stable. I remember when my stepdad and my mom split up when I was around 15 years old. The foundations were rocked at home and it was a big deal for me. Not a big deal for my sister and my brothers, but it was for me because I loved going home, I loved home, I loved family. And so once those foundations were rocked, it made me feel unearthed. So, maybe going to the gym, I was creating an extended sort of existence, belonging, even though I didn't want to be there to box. These were the only other people that were around to give me that family feeling. But, suddenly, I was looking at life without it.

Johnny's relationship with Brendan Ingle and boxing was always about much more than becoming world champion. It's hard to comprehend how life would ever be the same for Johnny.

It was hard. It was dark, it was hard. My problem was confidence. Once I got my confidence in boxing, I could go anywhere by myself. I didn't worry about anything. I didn't worry about being jumped. I didn't worry about what people were saying about me. All of a sudden, in a moment, my confidence had completely gone. My self-belief had gone.

It felt like he was now describing the Johnny Nelson that first turned up at the boxing club to just make some friends, but this time there was no Brendan Ingle.

I didn't know what I was going to do. Brendan was so important to who I was and even now, he shaped the man I am today. And again, it's not disrespecting my mum, my stepdad and my brothers and sisters. I'm not disrespecting them. What I'm saying is, he taught me stuff in a way that works for me and he shaped me to the guy I am today.

If Brendan was Johnny's anchor in life, linked by boxing, facing the prospect of it not being there anymore would have been terrifying.

I wasn't qualified to do anything apart from punching someone in the face so it was hard and it was dark. It really was a dark time and you've got to go through life's trials and tribulations to get through that dark time, because if you don't, the consequences of those are of an adult, not of a child. When you're a sportsman, people make excuses for you, for your behaviour. When you're no longer a successful sportsman, and you're just like everybody else on the street, your consequences are those of an adult, so therefore, you're going to suffer the consequence and pay the price. But I felt like a child again without Brendan and boxing.

Johnny has become a highly successful broadcaster in retirement so he found a way through this darkness, but the emotion on his face as he describes this time tells me how hard it was.

The hardest thing was actually accepting I was retired and being at peace with it. My other family, my boxing family, that's what was taken away from me and that's what proper blew my brain. I reckon it takes five years of retirement to get through that and why so many ex-sportspeople struggle. Drink. Drugs. Some kind of scandal. Some kind of depression. Divorce. Whatever. Because they are angry at everything else around them. Chip on the shoulder. Their relationships are dysfunctional because they always had something else to focus on. They've now got to go to Morrisons just like everybody else. They've got to queue up like everybody else. And I know it's an arrogance, but the reality of being mortal all of a sudden kicks in. And this is why a lot of sportsmen and women for the first five years, until they get through that period, or get used to that period, is why they will struggle.

I didn't disagree with anything Johnny said but I felt like there was something even more fundamentally crushing for him in retirement: He was saying goodbye.

Saying goodbye to the Johnny Nelson he had become when no one, including himself, believed he could get there. Saying goodbye to an extraordinarily special journey with Brendan Ingle.

There was a mourning in this.

Chapter 12

Johnny Nelson (Part 2)

J ohnny's story is different to everyone else's in this book, and if I'm honest, different to any other great sportsperson that I've ever heard of. It just doesn't fit the script of how we believe our great sportsmen and women are produced. Take as a comparison Johnny's stablemate at the gym in Sheffield, Prince Naseem Hamed. 'Naseem' was signposted as a possible great from a very early age – blessed with incredible natural ability and confidence, and then coached and moulded by Brendan Ingle to become a boxing superstar. That makes sense to us but nothing about Johnny's journey did. That's why I believe there is so much to take from Johnny when we look at how seriously he struggled while moving into retirement.

A sportsperson's attachment to the identity they have built up in elite sport has been a consistent theme throughout this book as they discuss their challenges in retirement – 'If I'm not this anymore, then what am I?' And this confusion is then coupled with a resistance to letting go of that identity in retirement. Paul Walsh's challenges around this were enormous but everyone I have spoken to has had this to some extent. This subject of identity feels on another level for Johnny. You see, his story isn't a boxing one, it is a life one.

Brendan Ingle was clearly a remarkable man who, through challenge after challenge, persisted with helping Johnny become a man. Granted, that eventually meant he became a great cruiserweight boxer but it was about so much more than that. It meant that Johnny found an identity, confidence, standing and purpose in life. Whatever happened in the ring, it never took anything away from what he was learning from Ingle about how to handle life – that really is very special. I believe that boxing has this wonderful characteristic as a sport, whereby impressionable young men and women enter the gym from often difficult backgrounds, and can be helped enormously to live good lives regardless of whether they go on to boxing greatness. The guidance they receive from coaches and the discipline of the sport can help them immeasurably. This was the same for Johnny but that relationship with Ingle became a huge anchor in his life. If ever there was a problem or something didn't make sense, who did he go to? Always Ingle. And everything that Ingle told Johnny would happen, happened. Even in the face of it looking utterly impossible, it happened. For a man in his twenties to have this sort of guidance is profoundly powerful, and his trust in Ingle would have been unbreakable.

Johnny's experience highlights the impact that professional sport has on moulding a sportsperson's dependency for that environment – it is all they have ever known. It is their home. Look at Johnny – when retirement came, he needed the gym and Ingle more than ever. Why? Because it is what his whole identity was based on. It is why he described feeling like a child again in retirement. The boy became a man within boxing, but then in a split moment in retirement, the man can become a boy again. The lifeline and safety net of that sporting environment was not going to be there anymore and that is terrifying. Yes, Johnny could visit the gym and have a coffee with Ingle but it would never be the same again. There would never be quite the same intensity to that relationship. So, you can understand why, in that moment, Johnny might question whether *he* would ever be the same again. Ingle and the entire community of the gym had been the making of Johnny Nelson. The confidence he had grown, the performances he had achieved and the happiness he had felt, it all centred on Ingle and the gym. How could Johnny not feel like he was about to fall off a cliff in retirement?

This is not unusual in professional sport even though Johnny's relationship with Ingle was a unique one. Sportspeople can feel a strong dependency for the environment that they have literally grown up in. Facing the outside world without it can be crippling. Remember what Johnny said about it:

> All of a sudden, in a moment, my confidence had completely gone. My self-belief had gone.

The simplistic and, in my opinion, naïve approach to this would be to say something like, 'Well, come on, it's time to move on.' To say that ignores the twenty or thirty years of conditioning and dependency that would have built up in the sportsperson. It is certainly not as simple as 'moving on'.

I come back to what I quoted earlier in the book from Andre Agassi about his retirement from elite tennis: 'It's like preparing for death.'

There's quite a bit to unpick from this sentence and a great deal of it applied to Johnny. When Agassi said this, he was actually referring to the uncertainty of what happens to you after you die as a comparison to the same uncertainty you face when approaching retirement. Johnny knew that his boxing career was over on a physical level. His knee was knackered and time was against him, he wasn't going to be able to get back to the standard he needed to. There was no uncertainty about it, it was a fact that he had to accept. To have that physical ability taken away from an elite athlete can be crushing but there is a finality to it. It is a medical reality. However, there was a far greater uncertainty looming over Johnny as he faced retirement. Let's take ourselves back to when Johnny first went to the gym – he hated boxing and wasn't very good at it. Remember what he said:

> I remember travelling on the bus to some of the amateur shows and the guys would be talking about knocking somebody out, how they're going to do it, and I'd be shitting myself, thinking, 'Oh my God, what?? I can never do that. I'm not good enough for that.'

He was a young adult with virtually no self-belief that he could box, and then even when he did reach a shot at the highest level, with his two world title fights, he blew it. He bottled it. The uncertainty of whether he would be good enough to become a world champion one day was enormous at that stage! If Johnny had been left on his own at this point in his career, he would very likely have walked away, but he didn't because of Ingle. As he said, 'I didn't want to let him [Ingle] down.' Where there existed uncertainty in Johnny's mind, Ingle filled it with certainty – 'You're going to win, lose, draw, but you're going to learn, and if you stick at it, you'll be a world champion.' And then... it happened; he became world champion in beating Carl Thompson. Imagine someone telling you for ten years that you are going to win the lottery and then you bloody do win it! Your trust and appreciation of that person would have no limits. That was Johnny with Ingle.

And from that moment, everything clicked for Johnny – he was unbeatable; confidence flowed out of him – he had arrived in the world. But he had arrived because of the influence Brendan Ingle had on him. And when we say 'he had arrived', this wasn't just as an athlete or boxing – it was as a person. All of a sudden, everything made sense in the world. Johnny knew where he fitted in and what he was all about as a person. All that uncertainty had been removed, but the process to achieve that had always had the cloak of support of Brendan Ingle. That was now gone. Could he be the same person without it?

At the same time, Johnny also talks about how in retirement his identity as a successful sportsman didn't apply in the world anymore. He was back on civvy street and having to live with the consequences of his decisions without the protection that his successful boxing career afforded him. This is where Agassi's quote means a bit more than just the uncertainty people face. There is an actual death – it is the death of an identity. Johnny says, 'And I know it's an arrogance, but the reality of being mortal all of a sudden kicks in.' You see, the definition of being mortal is that you are not immortal. Elite sportspeople do live in an artificial bubble that creates a feeling of immortality. They are capable of great things and it feels like it will last forever but... it doesn't. When that reality hits, there is a death of that person they thought they were. That is what Johnny is describing in retirement and why he said it takes five years to come to terms with that. Imagine telling a young sportsperson that it will take them half a decade to come to terms with their sporting career being over?!

For Johnny, the death of his identity as a great boxer would have been even harder because he was so defined as a person by his relationship with Ingle and the gym. The answers about what would come next would have to take a lot of soul searching and time. There was no preparation for this because it was about much more than qualifications and networking, and it was inevitable that there would be bumps along the road while he discovered who he was without the same support of his boxing gym. The fact that Johnny has forged a second successful career, in broadcasting, is of enormous credit to him. It also shows that even when the cord was cut from Brendan Ingle, the man that Johnny had become under his guidance was still there.

What a sport has given a sportsperson as a human being is something that is often overlooked. We are so focused on results and performances that we sometimes forget about the life implications within this dynamic. Johnny's story is very much about this but this exists on many levels for different sportspeople. Their sport has been where they have matured into adults; it is where they have formed their most meaningful relationships in life; it is where they have been allowed to fall and rise; it is where they feel most at home whether they have won, lost or drawn. Of course, that creates a dependency of sorts. I think we could all acknowledge that would be natural, and it is why the prospect of breaking it off can feel so terrifying for some.

Chapter 13

Clare Shine (Part 1)

Clare Shine is different to every other person so far in this book. You see, everyone else has had years of perspective on how retirement was for them. They have had time to consider the darkest points and how they happened, but for Clare it's different. I spoke to her less than two weeks after she had retired from professional football. Retirement was as fresh in her mind as it could possibly be.

Clare reached every level possible in professional football but there is so much more to her story than just goals and matches. The truth is that I have been keen to speak to her for a long while now and this book just provided a perfect excuse for it. The reason for that desire is that both Clare and I have been public about our issues with alcohol during our professional sports careers. When I first read about Clare's story, I immediately connected with it. I really admired her for being so open about it, especially while she was still playing and at such a young age. The bravery in that is not to be underestimated. The moment I saw that she was retiring, I was desperate to get her involved in this book.

It's important that I add some more context around some of Clare's struggles before we look at how she got to the decision to retire from professional football aged just 27. Back in 2014, when Clare was just 19 years old, everything seemed to be going great for her. She won Ireland Under-19 Player of the Year, got her first senior call-up to the Ireland team, and played in the Champions League for the first time. But it was also during this period that she broke her leg, and that's when things started to get bad. She spent a lot of time on her own during the rehabilitation process and then, when she rushed herself back to playing, felt a weight of expectation on her shoulders. Her mental health and relationship with alcohol seriously deteriorated and once where football had been her happy place, it was now full of darkness. Moves between Scotland and Ireland didn't do anything to help and everything was escalating in the wrong way. During October 2018, she reached this point:

> I was walking aimlessly around Cork City, full of pints and God only knows what else, thinking, 'Nobody will even care… just do it, just do it.' Tears were rolling down my face over the thought of wanting to end it all there and then. The truth is that there were plenty of similar nights in the run-up to that one.

That was Clare's rock bottom, but breakdown can often mean breakthrough and, sure enough, it was also a moment when she took the first tiny steps of a steep climb to get back to being healthy again. There were some falls along the way but she kept getting back up. As we spoke in September 2022, Clare was over two years sober and looked happy and healthy. It's where I started our chat.

> In sobriety, I'm excellent. It's probably the strongest I've been. I did have a little blip during the summer, just with the change of going back into pre-season and it being

really, really intense and getting back into the routine of full-time training. The days are half-nine to four every day. I'm not used to being around people that much and I like to do my own thing now. But it's completely manageable, which is amazing.

There was a real sense of ease about Clare as she spoke. She seemed at peace with the world. I recognised this as something you often see in healthy, recovering addicts. It's in sharp contrast to the chaos that they speak with during active addiction, but in a healthy recovery, there is often a newfound calmness about them. I thought this was really interesting bearing in mind Clare had only retired from football a few days previously, and it was a huge moment in her life.

I had been thinking about retirement for a long time but I've always had that 6-year-old inside me being like, 'Come on, you can do it, keep going with that dream.' And then it's weird when people say, 'Oh, you know when you know.' And during the summer, I spoke to the club and said I can't do this anymore. It's emotionally draining me, and after everything I've been through, I was like, I don't want to feel like this anymore. I know what it's like to feel really good and to go after the things that I know come naturally to me, yet football and professional sport are tearing me down and it shouldn't be like that.

There was just so much to take from this from Clare. She recognised that professional football, which was her passion, purpose and desire in life, was killing her and she needed to step away. That is an amazing sense of awareness and honesty.

> After my relapse in 2020, it kind of opened my eyes to a lot of other things that were going on in the world. Whereas I feel like when you're in professional sport, you're in a bubble, you don't actually live in the real world. Everything is done for you. All your flights, your accommodation, all paid for. There's responsibilities on yourself for performance, but everything else is done for you. You just have to show up and the training is there, the cones are out, you're being told what to do, your lunch is ready for you and then you're in the gym and someone is giving you a programme telling you what to do. And for me, that's the way that I lived my life completely. Whereas when I actually got into recovery, I had to take on a lot of responsibility myself and it just showed me the complete difference to the life that I was living and to the life I'm living now.

Clare is actually describing an awakening about who she is and what she's doing in life during her football career, which is really unusual. Think back to everyone else in this book – they are now looking back and reflecting on who they were during their careers with the benefit of years of hindsight, and have just about found a perspective on it all. The reason for that is that professional sport is all-consuming – it doesn't give you time to ponder where you are in life and who you are. Elite sport demands ALL of you and to stay in it, you need to stay consumed by it. There is no breathing space.

It was as if my mind was also telling me that your life could be completely different without football. But that was a scary thought because I didn't know anything else other than football. I've never been to university, never been to college. Writing my book was the first thing that I actually properly achieved outside of football, and it's my biggest achievement to date. And the opportunities that came with that, the whole process going through each chapter and reflecting back on my whole career and afterwards – it was exactly the same feeling as I had when I won the Cup Final. And I was like, 'Wow, can life outside of football actually give me these feelings as well?' It was as if I had attachment to the feeling that sport and the social aspect has given me.

What is very clear from Clare's story is that football and addiction went hand in hand. Football created pressure and alcohol created the numbness in her head to deal with that. That in turn caused a vicious, self-destructive cycle that she couldn't get herself out of.

I always knew that I could do it. I always knew I had the talent to push myself over the edge and push myself as hard as possible, but this came with a cost where I was bombing after games. And alongside that was the anxiety that I had before games because I would need to sleep properly for them but I would overthink every single possible thing you could imagine, and then not sleep well. I'm a bit of a perfectionist and I think most athletes are because they always want to be better, they're always striving for the next thing. But then this got really bad for me and it was obvious to people that I was really struggling. When it came to the football in the last two years, I spent most of the time crying and feeling like I had failed.

There was just so much in what Clare said that I identified with. I often felt in my career that I had this ability to push my own engine of effort or determination into the 'red' – sometimes to a level that others couldn't. It allowed me to compete with much more talented people and survive at that level. But there was a strange darkness to it. It meant I could achieve certain things but it also had a self-destructive element to it. Pressing the engine into red lived with Clare and me both on and off the pitch. It can't just be allocated to certain areas of your life; it lives with you in everything you do. It means that balance in anything is incredibly hard to achieve and post-match drinking binges are all part of it. So, in the end, it was our greatest strength but also our greatest weakness. Eventually that engine breaks, having been stressed so much. Yet in her recovery from alcoholism, remarkably during her career, Clare found a way out of this.

Football has been my identity for the last twenty-one or twenty-two years. I was so afraid and that's why I held on to it for so long when I could have probably retired at twenty-three or twenty-four. I was afraid that I'd lose everything. I'd lose that sense of community, sense of being wanted somewhere or being loved for my sporting abilities. Whereas now I'm getting that in different ways. That came through recovery and it came to me by being able to properly find myself and find my purpose outside of football. I have love for myself today.

Even with the ease that Clare talked about all of this, I knew that there had to have been a period of coming to terms with it all. Acceptance, or rather a battle with it, has been a common theme for everyone in this book.

I'd say that's just me closing the book completely now because it was hard for me to accept, because I had so many amazing memories playing football. You know, I travelled the world playing with girls that I grew up with. That's a dream come true to be able to do that. And so many people would lose their left arm to be in the position that I was in, and that was an acceptance thing. Until I was able to accept that my addiction did come hand in hand with football, I was never going to get out of that vicious cycle that I was in.

I believe in life that when acceptance arrives over a certain situation, everyone tends to move forward quickly from it. There is no more resistance to what needs to be done.

Yeah, it happened very fast. I actually spoke to the club on the Monday and I had retired by the Sunday. They knew it was coming, the management knew it was coming, everybody knew it was coming because I was so miserable. But it was just in football that I was miserable. And they could see that. They saw it in the dressing room, they saw how much I struggled. They saw the emotions that came out of me. In the back of their minds, they were like, 'You need to stop.' Even so, when it got to my final training session on the Saturday morning, it hit me: 'My God. I have to empty my locker.' I had to bring all my stuff home. And a part of me started questioning whether I was doing the right thing but when I got home, I started reading through my journal because I journalled everything and I knew I was doing the right thing. It's really easy to remember the happy moments. But then when you're happy, it's hard to remember the sad moments. But there were many more sad moments than happy moments for me.

Before Clare knew it, Sunday had arrived and it was to be her very last professional football match.

There was no pressure, there was no expectation. The demands were still there, but it was up to me. It was so weird, the shift in mood was huge. When Sunday came around, it was all fine. I just had my same routine. I was like, 'This is really cool, my last hurrah.' But there were cards in the dressing room, which started to make me feel emotional before the game. And then I was very close to the fans because of my role in the community and there were young girls, maybe 5 or 6 years old, and there were ten of them, and they all had handmade 'Thank you Clare' cards. And I just remember welling up. I didn't expect it to be like that. I was walking into the dressing room telling myself that I needed to pull it together. I put cold water on my face. I played the game and it was all ok but after half-time, it was really starting to get to me and I could feel the tears rolling down my face. Eventually it was my time to come off and I just completely broke down. Nothing can prepare you for that, even though I had accepted it long before it actually came.

I found this so interesting. Clare was in a position of total acceptance about retirement. She knew with 100 per cent surety that it was right for her, and yet there was still emotion and tears around. Why? This is something I am going to talk about in the second part of my looking at Clare's experiences.

What was so beautiful to hear in Clare was the transformation she has made in her recovery from alcoholism and the clarity that has given her in life while stepping into retirement.

I've always been afraid of the future up until the last six months. But now, I know what direction I want to go in, I know what I can bring to the table. I know I have the personality and work ethic to get me to where I need to be. I feel like I've lived so much of my life in fear but now in recovery I'm just going to throw myself into the deep end. What's the worst thing that can happen? I'm just going to face it. I can face everything and run or I can face everything and raise. And that's just the way that I go about everything now.

I guess with such clarity over the future, that beggars the question as to whether Clare will actually miss football.

I think I will. A part of me will always miss the banter, miss the girls, but it doesn't take away how it actually made me feel. You know, it's easy to remember scoring a hat-trick in a Scottish Cup Final, but then that same day, that same night, I ended up in hospital over having a panic attack. So it's like every high came with a very low moment because I couldn't find that balance in between. So when I got really high, I was always waiting for the low. It's why I found it really hard to stop drinking, I was afraid of the comedown. So, of course, I will miss being on the pitch and having that passion on the pitch and going into a tackle, scoring goals, and winning games, but I won't miss how it actually made me feel afterwards.

It felt like every time that Clare spoke, an absolute golden nugget of information came out of her mouth, and in many ways, she felt like the perfect last sportsperson for me to speak to for this book. There was so much she said that answered or encapsulated some of the mental struggles others have described in my conversations with them, and the interesting fact around this was that she has had less time to consider it all than the others. It was the clarity in Clare that was so intriguing.

There are two final quotes from Clare that I want to leave you with in this chapter. They are both very powerful when you consider everything that has been raised within this book. The first one is her answer to what she would tell her 16-year-old self:

I would tell her to do what makes her happy and make decisions for herself rather than for other people. I would tell her to believe in herself properly and truthfully, and just enjoy it and be present. Because football and sport is only a short career and for mine, even shorter, just to try and enjoy the moments rather than just being there and turning up for numbers.

And the second one is one of the last things that she said to me as we ended our conversation and said our goodbyes:

Yeah, I think the reason I'm feeling so good is because I know I have so much more to offer the world. I know that football is not my identity anymore.

The topic of 'identity' is something that this book has kept coming back around to with whichever person I have been speaking to and whatever story they have had. It just won't be ignored.

Just maybe, Clare's story is the one that best explains why.

Chapter 14

Clare Shine (Part 2)

Clare Shine stands on her own in this book.

The calmness and happiness that she spoke with when talking about retirement was at complete odds with the dark challenges that everyone else has spoken about. Where they have described fear and confusion, she has exuded happiness and optimism. Now, you might argue that's because she has only *just* retired and there is more to come. Well, maybe, but I'm not convinced. There was a sense of dread in everyone in this book, except for Clare, about making the decision to step away from their sport. For Clare, there was some sadness but definitely not big fear. Instead, she had a full acceptance of the decision that needed to be made and why. I cannot say this strongly enough but this is a profoundly important point when we look at the potential challenges athletes face in retirement.

Clare's story is very similar to mine and I'll build on this in the next chapter, but in short, she came to a realisation that the identity she was in football was killing her. It might have been producing goals and great performances but it was also driving her to major mental health and addiction issues. Remember what she said: 'Until I was able to accept that my addiction did come hand in hand with football, I was never going to get out of that vicious cycle that I was in.' Let's just look at that in isolation because that really is a big realisation. Football had been Clare's whole world for the best part of twenty years and she is still only 27 years old. Virtually her whole life was dominated by football. It was her first love, her dream, her passion, her purpose, her reason, her affirmation, her community... her everything. So, to reach a mental place that you realise that this massive thing in your life is going to kill you, is a HUGE moment. It is actually a moment that most other people simply won't understand. She was *choosing* to step away from the biggest thing in her life for what...? Well, the truth is she doesn't really know, but it needs to be something else other than playing football. Just read through those sentences again if it doesn't hit you how big that is. Take yourself back to one of the earlier chapters when I talk about the conditioning an Olympic athlete gets when they start their journey that I call the 'Road to Utopia'. Clare's conditioning around football was no different – it was the be-all and end-all in her life, but she broke out from it.

So, how did she come to this realisation? The hard truth is that it came about because she very nearly killed herself through substances or suicide. She reached a rock bottom that shocked her into wanting to get better. She knew she couldn't carry on the way she was going without something very bad happening so she chose recovery. Breakdown meant breakthrough.

These words from her say so much about her journey through recovery:

> When I actually got into recovery, I had to take on a lot of responsibility myself and it just showed me the complete difference to the life that I was living to the life I'm living now.

You might read this and simply see it as Clare's acknowledgement that she needs to take more responsibility in her life but it is much more than that. She is literally talking about making a fundamental change to who she is. That is massive. She is verbalising how in recovery, in order to stay healthy, she has to have a clear and obvious change as to how she approaches and handles life, and crucially, it needs to be completely different to how it is within football.

You see, the death of your identity as a professional sportsperson in retirement is as inevitable as death is for anyone in life, but this isn't always something that retiring sportspeople can see. Physically, you can't continue being an elite athlete forever; Old Father Time catches up with all of us. It's obvious that you can't continue entertaining tens of thousands of people through your sporting ability if you can't do it anymore and there are no crowds to watch. You can't remain the star of the show if you're not actually in the show! The death of that identity is going to happen whether someone likes it or not. That is why we have seen everyone in this book describe sadness or even mourning that they have felt at the end of their careers and, for some, a long time into retirement or even up until today. It is also why Clare felt so emotional during her last match. In those moments, you are saying goodbye to someone and that person is… YOU. That is incredibly difficult for 99.9 per cent of sportspeople and I will come back to this later in the book, but it wasn't that difficult for Clare. The reason for this is because that version of herself was, quite literally, killing her – she simply chose life. So, the happiness, calmness and acceptance I could hear in her was because she had no resistance to letting go of that professional footballer identity. In 'The Twelve Steps of Alcoholics Anonymous' (within *The Big Book*) they talk about there being a 'profound personality change' in someone who achieves recovery. Remember that when you read these words again from Clare:

> I feel like I've lived so much of my life in fear but now in recovery I'm just going to throw myself into the deep end. What's the worst thing that can happen? I'm just going to face it.

It was only by luck that I spoke to Clare after speaking to Johnny Nelson but it seems poetic now. The differences in how they viewed their identities within their sports and how they felt as they stepped into retirement couldn't have been greater. Johnny felt that his whole identity as a purposeful, healthy and successful human being had been built in the boxing gym with Brendan Ingle, whereas Clare could view the person she was in football as being a very unhealthy one. That is why when they stepped into retirement, one was fearful of what was next and one was delighted with what was next. There is a great lesson in this within the context of this book.

Clare's optimism about what was to come next in life after football was also born in her recovery from her addiction and mental health issues. She was not only happy to let go of the old version of herself in football but she had also started a relationship with a new person… HERSELF. In recovery, she has learned to love herself and be proud of what she can do *regardless* of football, and again, this is a profound change to where her head was at during most of her football career. Up to this change, everything was about football, including where she got her self-worth from. This is no different to almost all elite sportspeople – they define themselves by how they are getting on in the sporting arena. Clare's happiness was derived from how she was playing at football – when she was scoring goals and winning matches, all was grand in the world! Want proof of this? Well, look what happened to her when she broke her leg. Mentally she had nowhere to go. She was physically not able to do the thing that gave her a sense of self-worth in the world so she was left in a dark mental place. This happens to a lot of athletes when they suffer a major injury. Physically they are suffering but mentally they can suffer even more. So, one of the major aspects that has come from Clare's path in recovery is that she has discovered a newfound feeling of self-worth about who she is and what she is capable of in the world beyond football. Having been brought up in a world that was all about football, she reached a place of discovery that showed her that actually life is not all football. It's led to her not feeling fearful about what's next even though she doesn't know exactly what the next five to ten years will look like.

I believe that the reason Clare was able to come to this self-awareness is that she was actually given time during her football career to do so. That time came about because she was so unwell through her mental health and addiction issues that she needed time away from the game. She needed breathing space from the all-consuming world of football to understand what was happening to her. And this wasn't time afforded to her while recovering from an injury because during that time you are actually still in football. You are still at the training ground with the physiotherapist doing your rehabilitation every day – still in the bubble. Instead, Clare had a complete step away from football while she got better. This is a significant difference to someone who is living and breathing their sport throughout all of their career – they literally know no different. As painful as that time was for Clare, it gave her space to see a world beyond kicking a football. It gave her time to begin to understand and love herself better as a human being, not as a footballer. Take a moment again to think about how different this was for Johnny Nelson. He felt like Brendan Ingle and the boxing gym had discovered and made him. He had been there for twenty years and actually didn't want to leave because he was so interconnected with it. The boxing gym was him and he was the boxing gym. It was very hard, arguably impossible, for him to see a world beyond boxing that didn't terrify him. That wasn't because he was 'unprepared' for retirement, it was because of how he was conditioned as an athlete during his boxing career. Everything in life was boxing. He could have gone on a few different courses and picked up some qualifications that would have helped him earn money when he couldn't fight anymore but what would have helped him fit into another world that he felt completely lost in? I would say the only thing would be time and support from people around him to allow him to let go of the old version of himself and find the next. Remember Johnny said that he needed five years to do this. The contrast for Clare was huge because she had opened the window to see life beyond football while *still* a professional footballer, and that, in my opinion, is why she speaks with such peace about retirement in contrast to the others.

I feel that Clare's input into this book has been hugely significant. As I look back over the previous chapters from Matthew, Paul, Tom, Gail and Johnny, I can often see that they raise questions around the struggles of retirement that they can only partially answer. It is as if they are still processing it all in real time. It has all been such a huge experience for them that it has taken or is taking years for them to unpick it, whereas for Clare it's different. Her experiences are real-life examples to answer many of their questions. I suspect Clare will have created hurt in herself and others during active addiction that she wishes she hadn't. I was exactly the same. But, and it is a huge 'but', that chaos and pain allowed her to break through and find herself. Without any of it, she wouldn't be where she is today. And I want us to consider what her retirement might have looked like if she hadn't managed to find this self-awareness in recovery. It would have almost certainly been a forced retirement, i.e. it wouldn't have been her choice. She would have either been so unwell that she couldn't have continued or have behaved so badly that the game would have cast her out as a troublemaker. Either way, it wouldn't have been good. Importantly, she wouldn't have found peace with the decision. She would have still seen herself as a footballer, but just one not playing. All that clarity and calmness that she speaks with today would be replaced with confusion, resentment and even anger. The future would look very scary to her as she craved to be back playing football, where she felt she belonged. All of it would have created an even more dangerous cycle of behaviour, with some dire outcomes.

Due to my own story, I love seeing Clare happy and healthy. She now carries a very powerful message, which she knows, and is using to help others. But having spoken to her for this book, her message isn't just about addiction, it extends to how to handle retiring from professional sport. Looking at the alternative way Clare could have retired is sadly a look at what happens to many athletes.

Clare's experience has all been about letting go of the identity she held as a professional footballer and that seems to hold the key to it all.

Chapter 15

Me

Ok, I guess it would be remiss of me not to talk about my own experiences of leaving professional cricket and moving into retirement!

I have focused on all these other people and yet I have my own story to tell. I also believe my story can contribute, somewhat significantly, to this discussion. The reason why? Because, off the bat, I can tell you that my retirement years have been the happiest of my life. I haven't felt any fear and I haven't missed cricket, not one jot. Hand on heart, there has not been one aspect of leaving cricket that has upset me. Also, during this time, I got divorced, which is always difficult, but never did I feel destabilised by not being within my old cricket community. I can actually say that I have loved being away from my old life as a professional cricketer! I fully appreciate that this disclosure might blow your mind a little bit considering everything that we have discussed in this book. It might make you question why I am even writing it. I hear you say, 'So, this is a book diving into the challenges sportspeople face in retirement and yet the author says he faced zero difficulties?' Yeah, granted, it's a bit mad, but honestly, it is one of the reasons that I wanted to write this. A large chunk of my passion for writing comes from the adventure I find within a book. I am often on a personal journey of discovery myself while I write. I don't necessarily start with the answers and within my writing I seem find them – this process has been very much about that. I wanted to find out how others felt and why almost every retiring sportsperson faces massive challenges, while… I didn't. You see, from a personality and background point of view, I am most like Tom May from all the people featured here, and yet our experiences of transitioning into retirement have been completely different. Why? What is it specifically that has made such a difference?

I had set up a successful business before I retired from cricket and you might look towards that as the reason for my smooth transition. In fact, a lot of other ex-cricketers always mention that to me. I don't think that's true. In fact, I know that's not true. I don't think my healthy transition had anything to do with 'preparation'. To be honest, I think it is actually the opposite. You are going to need to bear with me on this but I know that my happiness in retirement has come from unpicking so much of what I learned and became while I was a professional cricketer. Like I said, bear with me and let me explain this more because I appreciate you might think this sounds crazy! I played elite sport and in order to be happy in retirement, I have had to unlearn so much of what I became in a high performance environment, and yet I still needed to be successful and earn money in retirement so why and how would I unlearn traits that could possibly help me with that? I know, it sounds back to front! There is real truth in this, though, and I need to take you back to when I retired from professional cricket.

My retirement announcement was in November 2011 and I had just spent four weeks in a rehabilitation facility with addiction and mental health issues. I had completely fallen apart as a human being at that point. I was having a breakdown of sorts while appearing to be 'successful' to the outside world. I felt like

I had broken into a million littles pieces. And the question that kept going around my head in rehab was: 'Where did it start and finish for me to end up in here?' I was to many people 'winning' in life and yet there I was, a complete shell of a man. I spent four weeks crying and soul-searching for how my life had got to this place. I didn't know how I'd got there or what to do next but what I did know in the very core of me was that I couldn't go back to what I was doing. I was ruining everything in my life – I was toxic. I wanted to find happiness. I wanted to be a far better version of myself.

After twenty-eight days of group and personal therapy sessions, it was very clear that if I wanted to have these things then I needed to CHANGE. And not a little bit of change; I needed to change everything. That started with me getting a fundamental understanding of who I truly was. I had to strip back all the bullshit I had told myself and others and get really honest with myself. Once I got there then I could truly change. This passage of discovery was both terrifying and illuminating. Sometimes I felt like I was jumping off a cliff into the unknown and other times it felt like I was being set free. What I realise now in looking back is that I was finally discovering who I truly was and what made me happy. The old structure of who I thought was me was being broken down. Crucially, I was discovering that much of what made me successful in cricket was actually making me into a person that I hated.

This bombshell discovery for me was hard to take. I had been a professional cricketer for fifteen years and had been acknowledged by others for being successful as a result. I had set up a business from scratch and made it successful. I had made my parents proud. Surely I *was* winning in life? Well, at 35 years old, I was sitting in a rehabilitation hospital with my life falling apart, and to understand some of it, I needed to understand all of it. Let me give you some examples.

As a professional cricketer, all I wanted to do was win. I wanted personal and team success, and I would do whatever it took to get that. I was absolutely relentless in that pursuit and I was no different to every other elite sportsperson in that way. Would I cheat to succeed in this pursuit? Hard truth – yes. There were many times that I pretended that I hadn't hit the ball, when I knew I had, and there were many times when I appealed to the umpire when I knew the batsman wasn't out. Now that might not be grand scale cheating, but cheating is cheating, right? It reflected my intensity to win. But importantly, in this pursuit, I wasn't just competing against the opposition, I was competing within in my own squad. Everyone was jostling for positions to get into the first team so when you secured a spot, you would do anything to keep it. It meant that training sessions could be just as important as matches. If I could look better than a teammate in order to get in the team, I would 100 per cent take that opportunity. I wouldn't necessarily say I would step over people to get to where I wanted but I certainly wouldn't catch them as they fell.

You might read this and come to the presumption that this is very normal in elite sport and the truth is that it is. It was a survival of the fittest mentality and I was not going to drown while others did. But over a long period of time, this mentality didn't make me healthy. I became obsessed with what people thought about me as a player and as a person. I would blend to whatever shape or personality you needed me to be if I felt that it would garner me support to stay in the team and do well. It was just the way I survived and, I guess, thrived in elite sport. *All* that mattered was winning and being successful. Within this pursuit, I completely forgot or lost who I actually was and what made me happy because that was all a side issue compared to whether I was winning. Yes, I got some happiness from winning, I'm not going to deny that, but it was brief and completely out of balance from reality. My whole identity and persona was based on whether I was being successful or being perceived as that by others; there was nothing fundamentally behind that. I relentless chased winning, blindly believing that it's what made me happy, so imagine how I felt when I found myself desperately unhappy. Nothing made sense to me. If I wasn't this person then who was I? I had been doing this for all of my adult life up till now. I realised that what had made me successful in cricket, i.e. a relentless chase for success and outside affirmation, didn't make me truly happy in life. There was something missing, a huge hole in who I was being in the world. If I was to fix this then I would have to find a different way to live.

Another example is how I dealt with pressure during professional cricket. I lived in a culture of boom and bust. The pressure of matches would be released by big alcohol blow-outs afterwards. It felt like the only way to recalibrate the hard work and tension that I had felt during the match. And you know what? There is truth in this and it works for lots of professional sportspeople, but for me, over time, it didn't. My blow-outs became extremely dangerous binges that I struggled to stop. I would behave in ways that shamed me to the core yet all under the guise that I was just 'letting my hair down'. As much as I was able to laugh this all off with bravado for a while, I couldn't keep that up. Over the years, that shame took its toll because deep down I knew that I was hurting people, including myself. The problem was that I didn't know any other way of handling and releasing the pressure that built up in me. My pursuit to win and survive in elite sport was unrelenting and without a way to open up the pressure valve inside me, I felt like I might explode, yet if I kept doing what I was doing, I was also destroying myself. It was a horrible trap to be in. As I gained time and sobriety in order to understand all this, I realised that I needed to find another way to handle pressure in life. Yes, the pressure came from cricket at this time, but the pressure actually came from how I was handling life in general. I needed to find a way to completely reset myself so that I didn't need to feel like the pressure was going to get too much for me and I would run to alcohol for an escape. As with all of it, this wasn't a quick fix, but I knew I couldn't go back to being that person I was in professional cricket.

A final example would be my relationship with control while a professional cricketer. I'm sure that having read what I have written in this chapter so far, it wouldn't surprise you that I was a complete control freak during my career. Being obsessed with outcomes meant that I felt like I needed to control every single aspect during the process towards that outcome. There was no room in my mind to just 'see how things go'. Once again, this is very common in elite sportspeople but for me, over time, it became very unhealthy. I was like the director of a theatre production who shouted at everyone to do what I said but when it all went wrong, I shouted at people for not listening to me enough. It was never really my fault. All of this just created pressure in my mind. I would have the same breakfast every single morning while I was on a winning run and if I had forgotten to buy that particular brand of bread, I would bark at my wife that she should have bought it. It was a completely unmanageable and unhealthy way to live life. So, to find another way, I needed to learn to let go of my control issues and have some faith in what may or may not happen, and importantly, be comfortable in dealing with whatever the outcome was – good or bad. This was all completely foreign to me within that persona that I had built in my mind as a professional cricketer.

I didn't play another game of professional cricket after leaving rehab and I will always be grateful for that. To try to fundamentally change my life while going back into an environment in which I had formed myself into a person that I didn't want to be would have been very difficult – maybe impossible. It meant that when the door was closed on my professional cricket career, another door opened for me to become who I truly was and find happiness in my life. This process of change involved me understanding what I needed to unlearn from my life in professional sport. Granted, this was about me finding a way to be healthy in life because of my addiction and mental health issues but there was something even more profound in this change that I needed to make. I didn't like the person I had become in professional cricket. It wasn't who I felt I truly was. It was the only type of person that I knew how to be at that point in my life but I was willing to do what I needed to do to walk away from that person. You see, I was tired of the shame that I lived with; I was tired of the lies and the manipulation; I was tired of the constant chase for other people's affirmations; I was tired of not feeling comfortable with who I was. I wanted out from that.

So, how did this all impact on my transition from professional cricket into retirement? Well, it actually made it really easy because I was happily walking away from that life and that person I was in that life. Even today, some eleven years on, I can get anxious with the thought of going to an event when I'm back to being a 'cricketer'. I don't go to any of the Old Player dinners or get-togethers, not because I don't like my old teammates – that couldn't be further from the truth – but because I feel like I could go back to being the old version of myself that made me really unhappy. Retirement has meant that I have had a natural way to find closure in that part of my life. That is why I relate so much to Clare Shine because she also wanted to let go of the identity of being a professional sportsperson because of where it was taking her. The strange thing is that I love cricket today as much as I did when I was a kid, but I don't miss playing it. I think, weirdly, that is because my mind associates playing with being that person I used to be and I don't want that. There is no question in my mind that a big chunk of the challenge that professional sportspeople face in retirement is because they find the 'letting go' process so difficult; they don't want to let go of that version of themselves. It was the exact opposite for me – I couldn't wait to be freed from that old Luke who was causing me and everyone around me so much pain.

The identity that a professional sportsperson has built themselves during their career is very powerful. It has allowed them to be successful in some highly pressurised and challenging situations. It has also allowed them to find a way back from setbacks and injuries. This identity would have been their anchor as to how to operate in elite sport. Not only would it be working for them but also for the people they are competing against – they can see it all around them. It is *their* environment. It is an identity of strength, dominance, resilience and, ultimately, success. Unlike me, almost every sportsperson will be in love with this identity. They will love what he/she has done for them whether that be through structure, discipline, ego, fame, money or confidence. It is powerfully intoxicating. So, now you can see why the change that retirement puts forward can be extremely difficult. Retiring sportspeople can see that life is going to be difficult and they are going to need to adapt, but do they consider that they will have to let go of the identity that they have built up and fallen in love with? In the vast majority of the cases, the answer is… no. I don't even think either Clare Shine or I had this awareness, rather it was forced on us by the necessity, or better phrased 'crap', that our lives had become.

Let me give you some examples to enable you to think about this. Matthew Hoggard knew exactly who he was and what he was meant to do in cricket. Paul Walsh loved the attention and notoriety that football gave him. Tom May understood the rules that rugby had taught him about life. Gail Emms was in love with the position that she achieved in life. Johnny Nelson had gone from a boy to a man, from a zero to a hero, during his boxing career. In retirement, they faced the reality that all of this had changed but they didn't want it to change. And the 'it' here is not the fact that they couldn't compete anymore, it was that they didn't want to change who they had become and how they operated in the world.

That is why in retirement from professional sport there is a death and there is a mourning that follows it, and for some people, this can last a long time. It is best described by the title of this book.

It is the death of you.

Chapter 16

Nature and Nurture

Should there really be any debate on whether a huge majority of elite sportspeople will find serious challenges in retirement? After everything that we have covered in this book, this answer has to be NO. It is a matter of 'when' rather than 'if', and to wrap up our understanding of this, we have to consider both the nature and nurture of an elite sportsperson. Let's begin with nature.

The average Joe doesn't become an elite sportsperson. It is called 'elite' sport for a reason. The characteristics within someone that help them reach the top of their sport will always have been there. In some cases, for example Johnny Nelson, they take a little longer to emerge, but they are always there. That person will have certain physical abilities and for some, those will be very significant, but far more importantly, that person will have exceptional mental abilities. Most prominent within that will be their ability to hyper-focus. They will focus on what they want and it will be impossible to break them away from that. That focus will centre on self-obsession – it is about what *they* want, and outside of that, little else will matter. It is why elite sportspeople can be a nightmare to live with because selfishness is a huge part of who they are. In many ways, it is a necessity for them. They require a level of selfishness that will prevent them from being overtly distracted by the emotion or needs of others. I'm certainly not trying to make out elite sportspeople are monsters but you only need to ask the partner of one to find out how difficult they can be – many a family event will be disrupted because the athlete feels they need to rest or train or do something else that is going to help them. Everyone fits around them, not the other way around.

This type of character will therefore live in quite an abnormal world. They are effectively living the life of being someone 'special', or at least that is the way they are being treated. The average Joe doesn't have his or her family dancing to their beat and knowing that their needs will come second to the athlete's almost every single time. Now, imagine this happening from a very young age, all the way through the teenage years, and then throughout adulthood until the end of a sporting career is reached. Are we seriously expecting an athlete not to have solidified that characteristic of self-obsession within them by the time they retire? They are not trying to be a nasty person but that level of selfishness, which has given them the ability to laser-focus on what they want to achieve in a sporting arena, is not going to disappear suddenly. But there is a major change now. The challenge the athlete faces in retirement is that they are looking at a world outside of sport that doesn't like that characteristic. They are no longer seen as particularly 'special' and people around them won't be prepared to fit their lives around them or let them get away with types of behaviour they have expressed so far in their life. This is even more prominent in a new working environment the athlete may step into. For example, during their sporting career an athlete has essentially been their own boss. Consider a boxer standing in the corner ready to fight as the bell goes. There is no one holding their hand in that moment – it is up to them to deliver under extraordinary pressure. That is why high-performing athletes will be exceptional at taking on personal responsibility, but the flipside is that they will want things to be as they feel they need to be for them to perform at their best. We can't have it both ways with them. We cannot expect it all to be on their shoulders at crunch time and not expect them to demand certain things to be right for them.

Consider this personality now in a more normal working environment. They are very likely to want structure and organisation to fit around them so that they can 'perform'. If someone has a style of working that doesn't suit them then they are going to look to that person to bend for them rather than the other way around, but why would we expect anything else? The nature of an elite sportsperson, the make-up of the personality that helped them achieve huge sporting successes, is going to run headfirst into the real world in retirement. There is no way around this. There aren't enough educational courses that they can go on to avoid this happening. Look back on everyone I have spoken to for this book, they have all had that moment of 'Oh shit, this is how it is now', and that has always come as a shock to them. It is a 'life changed the rules but no one told me' type of moment! Sometimes this can be lazily described as 'having an ego', but again, I'm not sure what we are expecting from our top sportspeople. That ego has made them very successful, so how are they going to switch that off at the drop of a hat to fit in easier with the world outside of elite sport? Simple answer – they can't.

Now let's move on to nurture, which we have already touched upon within the paragraphs on nature. The world in which a sportsperson grows up and the conditioning they receive during that time is absolutely fundamental to what we are talking about. Look at every single person that has contributed to this book –

they all knew where they stood in their sport. They knew how they were meant to behave, what type of attitude they needed and what the rules were on how to achieve success. That mental conditioning was reinforced in them day after day after day. There are slight variations in how this sat with each of them but, without exception, they have all talked about understanding the world they lived in within elite sport. The easiest example to illustrate this is how they dealt with something not going well – a loss or a bad performance. The environment that they had lived in since a young age told them that to move forward from this loss required honesty, personal responsibility, analysis, and crucially, a new plan. The people around them, teammates and coaches, knew that as well, so trust existed between them. They all had a bad day at the office but they knew how to move forward – simple. If you have existed in that environment for more than two decades, how on earth would anything different to that sit well with you? How would you find a culture of people making excuses or cutting corners? How would you find a culture of people not being honest with themselves and therefore repeating the same mistake over and over again? How would you understand a culture in which you suddenly felt like you couldn't trust the people around you? It would feel horrendous – a personal affront to their system of values, perhaps. The athlete in question could actually react quite aggressively about it all because it would feel so very wrong to them. They wouldn't respect the people around them or the structure that everyone was working in. Again, their nature would tell them that everyone else needed to change rather than themselves in order to make this work better. The reality is that the vast majority of the real world doesn't operate like elite sport. Remember what Tom May said on this – he suddenly felt like he was working in a world with multiple agendas that he knew nothing about. Gail Emms and Matthew Hoggard talked about never receiving feedback on how to move forward. That, again, is an affront to how they had operated in their lives up to retirement. It is no wonder why so many retiring athletes want to stay within their sports. Obviously, this is partly because it is a sport they love but it is also because it is an environment in which they were nurtured and understand so well.

I asked you at the start of this book to look at the reasons why an elite sportsperson finds retirement so challenging as a smorgasbord of issues, and I hope I have shown you that. Different personalities have different issues – from Matthew Hoggard, who feels abandoned without some structure around him, to Johnny Nelson, who feels the basis of everything he has become was in the boxing gym. However, there is one overriding point that encapsulates all of the issues I have brought to you with both my own and Clare Shine's stories. Without question, the biggest differentiator between someone who eases into retirement and someone who struggles with it is how quickly they can let go of their old identity. If you are a Cristiano Ronaldo, then you don't need to because you will always be a megastar, but he is in the tiniest percentage of elite sportspeople in the world. For the rest, they have to say goodbye to who they were and the world they lived in and be ready to start all over again. For Clare Shine and me, this was easy, we wanted to do it, but for people who don't have those problems, it will be far harder. This doesn't mean saying goodbye to the brilliant attributes that made them successful in sport but it does mean saying goodbye to the old identity who used them. The world outside of sport doesn't just feel different, it is different, and retiring athletes are going to have to adjust to it rather than the other way round. That concept will feel completely foreign to them bearing in mind their nature and nurture – it's not a simple process.

How quickly a retiring athlete can get their head around this will make an enormous amount of difference to the time it will take for them to feel at ease in retirement. The sad thing is that for some, they will never be able get to this place and issues will follow them around. Their previous identity can be something they so love and adore that saying goodbye to it never feels like something they want to do. They would prefer to try to make the outside world bend to them still, but it unfortunately won't. So, they encounter difficulties with mental health and addiction as they find life extremely difficult to cope with. It can be desperately sad to see and can often be misinterpreted as poor behaviour or 'having too much money', but underneath it all is a human being struggling to accept that their old life is no longer viable. As a contrast, the athletes who quickly move into a happy life in retirement understand that they are now going to have to reinvent themselves. That can feel daunting after years and years of working to 'make it' in sport, but the reality is that it needs to be done.

The tug-of-war between an athlete's old and new life is the key to this whole discussion and it prompted me to think about what I would tell a retiring athlete today. This is what I came up with:

> Savour the last moments of your career because they are a celebration of all the hard work and dedication that you have put in over the years. I know there will be

some sadness there because it is a time to say goodbye but alongside that feel happy and proud. You really have accomplished so much. The world outside of sport will be different and it is going to take some getting used to. It will feel hard at times and you might long to be back in your sport, where everything felt so much simpler, but times are changing, my friend!

Above all else, I want you to remember this – let go of being an 'elite sportsperson' – you are no longer that. Close that door now. It doesn't mean that you're not still brilliant in many things but you no longer live within that bubble of sport. YOU are going to have to change to fit with this new world, it will not move to you. YOU are going to have to start again in retirement. Don't feel scared by this – trust me, it's very exciting. You are going to find a second life that is as fulfilling as your first one as a sportsperson, but to do that, you have to let go of the first life. Be bold, be humble, and grasp the opportunities ahead of you. Not many people in life get to experience brand-new starts but you can do that now. Let one door close as you open a new one.

Acknowledgements

Matthew Hoggard, Paul Walsh, Gail Emms, Tom May, Johnny Nelson and Clare Shine – thank you so much for your time and honesty. This book is nothing without your personal stories.

My family – I treasure your unwavering support in allowing me to fulfil my enormous passion for writing. Long may it continue until someone asks me to stop!

Jonathan Wright and everyone at Pen & Sword and White Owl Books – without the ability to publish, all my books would sit as ideas in my head. Thank you for believing in me.

To all former athletes struggling in retirement – I hope this book gives you a voice and some inspiration to battle through the tough times you are facing. There is a lot more to life than just your sport.

Back from the Edge

Mental Health and Addiction in Sport

- Brutally honest account of a professional cricket player's battle with addiction
- Full account of treatment received at The Priory
- Looks at how sportsmen and women are highly likely to struggle with obsessive behaviour
- Warns of the need for more to be done to help young sport stars

The truth is that professional sport is a breeding ground for addictive behaviour.

Luke Sutton is a business owner and successful agent to sporting stars such as James Taylor, Nile Wilson and Sam Quek, but his life didn't always look so positive.

Back from the Edge reveals the huge ups and major downs that a professional career in sport can bring – and the mental health difficulties that can plague a sportsperson along the way. Luke knows this more than most. Brutally but refreshingly honest, this no-frills autobiography of the former professional cricketer describes in detail the moment he hit rock bottom, how he got there, his rollercoaster journey through rehab, and the important lessons he's learnt since.

Throughout the book, Luke remains candid and reveals how his addictions affected his personal life, from his friends to family to his children. *Back from the Edge* is heart-wrenching.

It's also thoroughly genuine, funny and utterly inspirational, and has allowed the former cricketer to speak about his mental health and to raise awareness of addiction in sport. Now a sports agent, he is perfectly placed to spot the warning signs in young stars, and to support them before they spiral into the same type of experiences he faced.

White Owl Books
ISBN: 9781526767547
RRP: £12.99

The Life of a Sports Agent

The Middleman

- Delves deep into the relatively unknown world of a sports agent
- Insight into the lives of well-known athletes from a variety of sports

There is a lot of mystery that surrounds sports agents and their roles in the lives of their high-profile clients. Many perceive the life to be glamorous, spending time with celebrities and earning a lot of money for doing easy or very little work. *The Life of a Sport's Agent* reveals how very wrong this perception is.

Having been a high-profile sports agent for nearly ten years, with clients such as James Anderson, Sam Quek, Nile Wilson, James Taylor and Simon Mignolet, Luke Sutton has an incredible insight into the world of sports management across a number of areas. In this book, Luke reveals stories and personal experiences about the sporting stars he has encountered, both the good and bad, and his very honest opinions about them.

The book also aims to give people a true look into how this mysterious industry works, and highlights the important lessons Luke has learnt during his career. *The Life of a Sport's Agent* follows Luke's 2019 autobiography, *Back from the Edge*.

White Owl Books
ISBN: 9781526736994
RRP: £12.99

Welcome to the
Wonderful World of Wicketkeepers

- Reveals what it is really like to be a wicketkeeper
- Full of humour, sadness and extraordinary insight from a professional wicketkeeper
- Includes stories from Jos Buttler, Jack Russell, Sarah Taylor, Alec Stewart, Chris Read, Amy Jones and Geraint Jones

The journalist Suresh Menon once said, 'You don't have to be mad to be a wicketkeeper, but it helps.' Wicketkeeping is one of the great arts of cricket on which, seemingly, everyone has an opinion and yet few really know what they are talking about. The wicketkeepers themselves are an eclectic mix of extroverts and introverts all trying to do the same thing every time they walk onto a cricket field – be perfect.

Welcome to the Wonderful World of Wicketkeepers is a book written by a wicketkeeper, Luke Sutton, which lifts the lid on what being a wicketkeeper is really like. This is not a dull, technical examination of the art but instead a look into the minds of the best who have done it in England. There is humour, sadness and extraordinary insight as Sutton allows the likes of Jos Buttler, Jack Russell, Sarah Taylor, Alec Stewart, Chris Read, Amy Jones and Geraint Jones to tell their own stories about what it truly means to be a 'keeper'.

White Owl Books
ISBN: 9781526784780
RRP: £14.99